D0283041

Choose Your College Major in a Day

Credits and Acknowledgments: I am extremely grateful to the economists, data analysts, and editors at the U.S. Department of Labor and the U.S. Census Bureau. These authoritative sources provided the economic information that appears in this book. Other occupational information is derived from the O*NET database, which was developed by researchers and developers under the direction of the U.S. Department of Labor. I used release 19 of the O*NET database, the most recent version available. The U.S. Department of Education developed the taxonomy of college majors and other educational and training programs (the Classification of Instructional Programs) that is used here. We are very fortunate to be living in a nation that makes available such rich sources of information.

LAURENCE SHATKIN, PHD

CHOOSE YOUR
COLLEGE
MAJOR
IN A DAY

Meyer & Meyer Media

British Library Cataloguing in Publication Data

A catalogue record for this book is available from the British Library.

Choose Your College Major in a Day
Maidenhead: Meyer & Meyer Media (UK) Ltd., 2015
ISBN: 978-1-78255-067-9

All rights reserved, especially the right to copy and distribute, including the translation rights. No part of this work may be reproduced—including by photocopy, microfilm or any other means—processed, stored electronically, copied or distributed in any form whatsoever without the written permission of the publisher.

© 2015 by Meyer & Meyer Media (UK) Ltd.
Aachen, Auckland, Beirut, Cairo, Cape Town, Dubai, Hägendorf, Hong Kong, Indianapolis, Manila, New Delhi, Singapore, Sydney, Tehran, Vienna

Printed in the United States of America
ISBN: 978-1-78255-067-9

Email: info@m-m-sports.com
www.m-m-sports.com

WHY YOU'RE GOING TO LOVE THIS BOOK

A college degree is usually viewed as the entry ticket to a career. That's why choosing a college major and choosing a career are two sides to the same decision. And that can be a tough decision to make.

That's where this book can help. It helps you choose a four-year college major based partly on the characteristics of majors and partly on the characteristics of the related careers. It identifies college majors that align well with your interests, your skills, and your experiences in high school. You'll find fact-filled but easy-to-read descriptions of majors and careers. And the book will guide you through a systematic process for reaching a decision.

But can you really make a decision within 24 hours? That's up to you. If you hole up with this book for a day, you can work your way through the exercises and facts and reach a tentative choice before the day is done. However, I hope you'll take additional time to explore your choice further and confirm that it is right for you.

This book may suggest a major or a career that you have not previously considered. Or it may confirm your previous plans. Either way, you'll gain insights into what you might study and what careers your studies might lead to. Just be sure to keep an open mind. You'll get inspired!

The book provides the two kinds of information that you need to decide on a college major:

❭ Information about you, to answer these questions: What satisfies you? What are you good at?
❭ Information about your options, to answer these questions: What will you study in various college majors? What careers do the majors lead to?

To help you get answers, this book leads you through a logical process:

Chapter 1	**What Is a College Major, and What Goes Into My Decision?** This chapter tells you what to expect in a bachelor's degree program, no matter what your major is. It identifies some of the important factors that differentiate one major from another, such as course requirements and career outcomes. It also explains what aspects of yourself you will consider in the next three chapters so you can make a wise decision.
Chapters 2–4	Each of these chapters leads you through a quick exercise that identifies your important needs, preferences, or abilities. You'll consider your personality type, your skills, and your favorite high school courses. At the end of each chapter, you'll see the names of college majors that may suit you based on what you've learned about yourself. You'll jot down the names of several majors that look promising.
Chapter 5	**What Are My Lists Telling Me?** In this chapter, you'll review the college majors that you have jotted down in the previous chapters. You'll look for patterns that indicate which majors deserve further exploration. You'll make a Hot List of the most promising majors.
Chapter 6	**Descriptions of College Majors.** This chapter offers important facts about 61 bachelor's degree majors: course requirements, high school prerequisites, specializations, and related career paths.
Chapter 7	**Descriptions of Careers.** This chapter describes all 161 occupations that are referred to in chapter 6, plus 100 job specializations. For each, it gives a definition, earnings, job outlook, top skills, personality type, and work conditions. It indicates when an additional degree beyond the bachelor's is necessary.

Chapter 8	**Deciding and Implementing.** This chapter helps you fill out a checklist that organizes your decision. You assign pluses and minuses to the majors on your Hot List so you can reach a tentative conclusion. Finally, it explains the issues you'll need to deal with when you implement your decision.
Appendix	Here you can find definitions of the personality types and skills used in chapters 2 and 3.

This book focuses on popular college majors. Understand that it does not cover every possible major. If you can't find the major you're looking for, look at the index. For example, if you're looking for the Spanish major, you'll find that the index directs you to the Modern Foreign Language major.

The book is limited to undergraduate bachelor's degree programs. For many careers, the usual entry route requires you to get a master's or doctoral degree, experience in a related occupation, or on-the-job training. You'll find information about any such additional requirements in chapter 7.

The majors in this book are linked to career outcomes that are considered the most typical, but understand that many people follow atypical pathways. For example, someone might earn a bachelor's in a scientific field and then complete a master's in business administration (MBA), with the goal of pursuing a career in technical sales or entrepreneurship. Another person might major in computer science as an undergraduate and then earn a graduate degree in a field that uses computers heavily, such as library science, management information systems, or actuarial science. Graduates with backgrounds in two different fields may be particularly attractive to employers.

It is also possible to get educational credentials in two fields by completing the requirements for a minor or a second major. See chapter 1 for details.

I wish you good luck with your decision and with the education that it leads to.

Descriptions of Related Occupations 144

CHAPTER 1

WHAT IS A COLLEGE MAJOR, AND WHAT GOES INTO MY DECISION?

Before you choose a major, be sure you understand what this commitment means and how to approach it in a thoughtful manner. If you're really pressed for time, you may skip this chapter, but many readers will want to skim it, at least.

WHY DO I HAVE TO DECLARE A MAJOR?

The simplest answer to this question is that most colleges require it. Some offer a general studies major for those who are unable or unwilling to commit to a particular program of study. But you probably are reading this book because you want to prepare for a particular career or at least concentrate on one field of knowledge, so you want to commit to a specific major.

At most colleges, you declare your major by the end of your sophomore year. However, you can benefit from having a specific major in mind before then: You can try out introductory courses and get a taste for the subject that the major focuses on.

In fact, it can be very helpful for you to have a major in mind while you're still in high school and deciding which colleges to apply to. Some colleges are better places than others to study certain majors because of factors on which they excel, such as their course offerings, the experience of their instructors, their research facilities (libraries and laboratories), or their connections with employers. Having a major in mind while you're in high school also can help you choose high school courses that will prepare you for the program you'll enter in college—for example, taking math as preparation for a science major.

WHAT IS A MAJOR?

A major is a program of study that meets certain requirements. Usually the major is defined by the department offering it (for example, English by the English department), but some interdisciplinary majors have a focus that bridges several departments.

Most colleges and universities impose several different kinds of requirements for majors:

> **Requirements for all degree candidates.** These are courses (and, in some cases, experiences such as internships) that the college wants everyone to take in order to get a well-rounded college education rather than just narrowly focused career preparation. For example, many colleges expect all bachelor's degree candidates to acquire some background in math, natural science, social science, and the humanities. Students usually have considerable freedom in choosing courses to meet these area requirements. If a required subject seems challenging or uninteresting to you, often you can meet the requirement with an introductory or survey course. Sometimes you can choose between a bachelor of arts (BA) or a bachelor of science (BS) degree; the BS degree usually has fewer area requirements. Some fields have highly specialized bachelor's degrees, such as a bachelor's in engineering (BEng). Most colleges also require you to maintain a certain minimum grade-point average and show progress toward completing some kind of degree. You won't get by on a "partyology" major.

❭ **Requirements to enter the major.** Some majors are open to everyone who enrolls at the college, but for other majors, certain relevant high school courses must be on your transcript. Still other majors require you to complete a year or two of college before being admitted, during which time you must complete prerequisite courses. For example, to enter an engineering program, you may need to take calculus and physics courses. Your overall grade-point average or perhaps the grades in prerequisite courses may need to be above average.

❭ **Requirements to complete the major.** In most majors, you take a combination of courses from within the department and from other departments. For example, in an agronomy program you would study plant nutrition and weed control and also chemistry, genetics, and statistics. Toward the end of the program, you may need to participate in some kind of supervised hands-on experience or show your ability to do research by completing a senior project or thesis. In some very career-oriented programs, a professional association specifies what all colleges should require, but major requirements in most fields vary from one college to the next. Don't assume that your college requires exactly the same courses listed in chapter 6 of this book.

❭ **Concentrations within the major.** Often it is possible to choose a specialization within a major. Sometimes it's required. For example, students majoring in theater arts may need to choose a concentration in directing, acting, design and technical theater, or playwriting. Each concentration has its own course requirements beyond the core courses that everyone in the major must take.

WHAT DOES IT MEAN TO CHOOSE A MINOR OR A DUAL MAJOR?

Students choose a minor or dual major for several reasons. Some students are interested in two fields and want to explore both to some extent— maybe not in equal depth. Some students want to impress future employers by showing that they have a diverse set of skills, not just those associated with one major. They may be aiming for a high-paying niche career, such as the market researcher who is knowledgeable about a foreign culture or the computer network manager who can do a sophisticated statistical analysis of LAN traffic. Still other students want to take a chance on building a career in a field that interests them and, at the same time, acquire credentials for a "plan B" field in case their main interest turns out to be impractical in the job market. All of these reasons are valid.

The requirements you complete for a minor will give you a reasonable amount of background in the subject without covering as much ground as the requirements for the major. You could construct your own program of courses to become skilled in a subject outside of your major, but when possible, it's better to have the formal credential of a minor on your transcript.

Meeting the requirements for dual majors is easiest when the two subjects are fairly similar and certain courses can serve both majors. On the other hand, students who want to pursue a dual major often have diverse interests with little overlap. In such cases, completing two majors can be tricky. Some required courses may not be offered every semester, so fitting them into four years may not be easy.

You should talk with an academic advisor no matter what your plans are for your major, but it is especially important to have this discussion if you want to elect a minor or dual major. You need to find out whether your plan will be practical and map out a path for completing it.

WHAT IF I HAVE TO CHANGE MY MAJOR?

You may want to—or need to—change your major because you have lost interest in it or are earning low grades. Doing this may prolong the time it will take you to get your degree, because your new major will impose its own set of requirements. Unless the new major is closely related to the old major, a lot of the course work you have completed will not count toward your new goal. You can avoid a setback of this kind by opting for a new major with very few specific requirements, but rightly or wrongly, most majors of that kind are not highly prized by employers.

You probably will need to work with an academic advisor to change your major, and this person usually will have access to a computerized "degree audit" that can analyze your transcript and show you how close you are to completing the requirements for various other majors.

The best strategy is to make a wise choice the first time you select your major, and that is one of the goals of this book. But if you have to make a change, the sooner you do so, the less ground you'll lose.

WHAT FACTORS SHOULD I CONSIDER WHEN SELECTING A MAJOR?

Here are the most important questions you should ask yourself when selecting a major:

〉 Will I be **successful** in the major?
〉 Will I **enjoy** the major?
〉 Will I be prepared for a rewarding and enjoyable **career**?

This book is organized to help you answer all three questions, with exercises that provide insights into your abilities and interests, together with information about career outcomes.

But don't overlook some other practical considerations.

Time and **expense** are two related issues that you should keep in mind. Some careers, such as medicine, law, and teaching at the college level, require you to get an advanced degree. Many managerial roles are within reach only after several years of work experience, during which you become knowledgeable about an industry and acquire the people skills that college courses rarely cover. You need to consider whether you will have the ability, funds, and persistence to keep on track for the many years it will take you to reach your career goal.

Competition is another issue that you should not overlook. Highly rewarding occupations tend to attract many jobseekers. This is true whether the chief reward is high income (for example, think of medicine) or simply prestige (think of the arts).

The competition may begin long before you hit the job market: Many postgraduate programs and even some undergraduate majors admit only a limited number of students, rejecting those whose grades or test scores are not outstanding. In professional programs, such as medical or veterinary school, those few who are admitted must work hard but rarely flunk out. In some doctoral degree programs, however, only the highest-achieving students may be allowed to proceed beyond the master's degree level, and competition for fellowship aid is often intense.

Chapter 6 of this book lists the typical requirements for each major, but the information can give you only a very rough idea of how much competition you will face as a student. Before you elect a major, talk to people who are already enrolled and who are successful in it. Get an idea of how your grades and test scores measure against theirs.

The occupational descriptions in chapter 7 can provide insights into the level of competition in the job market. The figures for workforce size, projected job growth, and projected job openings indicate whether the occupation will have high or low demand for workers. As for the supply of job candidates who will compete for these openings, be sure to look in the "Career Paths" statement in chapter 6 for any clue to the level of competition or the factors that are advantageous to jobseekers, such as a particular specialization or type of training.

But understand that these nuggets of information are based on national averages. Competition may be more or less intense where you live. Talk to local people who are working in the industry. Ask them what it takes to succeed. (Sheer determination and grit may be as important as a transcript with high grades.) If you foresee a small but significant chance that you won't succeed, think about what would be your best options for an alternative career goal. Many people find fulfillment in a "plan B" career. For example, I'm happy that my original plan for a career in teaching college courses did not work out, because a career of researching and writing has proved to be much more rewarding.

KEY POINTS OF CHAPTER 1

❯ In a major, you learn skills and knowledge related to one subject, but you also take courses in other departments and may even pursue a minor or second major in another subject.

❯ It's best to choose a major where you will succeed and find satisfaction, because changing your major may set back your graduation date.

❯ Be realistic about your ability to deal with the time, expense, and level of competition that you will face before you complete college and reach your career goal. Use information from this book and also from personal contacts.

CHAPTER 2

WHICH MAJORS MIGHT SUIT MY PERSONALITY?

People are most happy and successful when they are in situations where they fit in. This applies to college academics just as much as it applies to social gatherings and workplaces.

Which college majors would be a good fit for you? The answer depends on several factors: your interests; your abilities; the learning environments where you feel comfortable (lecture hall? laboratory? library?); and the careers that the major leads to.

Many psychologists have found that these factors tend to cluster together in constellations that can be described as **personality types**. For example, people with the Social personality type are interested in (and good at) helping other people; they learn well in collaborative environments; and they are successful in careers that involve teaching or providing care for others.

The psychologist John L. Holland described six personality types that characterize college majors and the careers they lead to: Realistic, Investigative, Artistic, Social, Enterprising, and Conventional. (If these titles are not very meaningful to you, read the definitions in the appendix.) Holland advised people to identify one of these personality types as their **primary** type, plus perhaps one or two **secondary** types.

Perhaps you have already done an exercise that has identified your personality profile. If so, you can skip ahead to page 38 and see the majors that are linked to it.

Otherwise, you can do the following exercise. It's a simple checklist to help you think about your personality. Because most people go to college to prepare for a career, it asks you about work activities rather than about the classroom.

This exercise is not a test. There are no right or wrong answers. There is no time limit, but it takes most people no more than 25 minutes.

1. For each work activity, think about whether or not you would like performing the activity.
2. Try not to think about how much money you would make performing the activity.
3. Use a check mark to indicate each work activity you would like doing.
4. Don't stop to count the check marks until you reach the end, where it says "NOW COUNT."

Which of these activities would you like doing?
(Check as many as you want.)

☐ Build kitchen cabinets
☐ Operate a dairy farm
☐ Drive a taxi cab
☐ Raise fish in a fish hatchery
☐ Catch fish as a member of a fishing crew
☐ Spray trees to prevent the spread of harmful insects
☐ Operate a motorboat to carry passengers
☑ Set up and operate machines to make products
☐ Guard money in an armored car
☐ Lay brick or tile
☑ Repair household appliances
☑ Install flooring in houses

- ☐ Enforce fish and game laws
- ☐ Work on an offshore oil-drilling rig
- ☐ Do cleaning or maintenance work

Go on to the next block of activities.

(For later: Total number of check marks for this block: ③ = **your R total**)

Which of these activities would you like doing?
(Check as many as you want.)

- ☐ Develop a new medicine
- ☐ Study ways to reduce water pollution
- ☐ Determine the infection rate of a new disease
- ☐ Diagnose and treat sick animals
- ☑ Conduct chemical experiments
- ☑ Investigate crimes
- ☐ Examine blood samples using a microscope
- ☐ Study the structure of the human body
- ☐ Study the governments of different countries
- ☐ Do laboratory tests to identify diseases
- ☐ Make a map of the bottom of an ocean
- ☐ Study rocks and minerals
- ☐ Study the personalities of world leaders
- ☐ Investigate the cause of a fire
- ☑ Develop psychological profiles of criminals

Go on to the next block of activities.

(For later: Total number of check marks for this block: ③ = **your I total**

Which of these activities would you like doing?
(Check as many as you want.)

- ☐ Design artwork for magazines
- ☐ Direct a play

- ☐ Perform comedy routines in front of an audience
- ☐ Write reviews of books or plays
- ☑ Act in a movie
- ☐ Draw pictures
- ☐ Sing in a band
- ☑ Edit movies
- ☑ Write stories or articles for magazines
- ☐ Play a musical instrument
- ☐ Dance in a Broadway show
- ☐ Sing professionally
- ☑ Create special effects for movies
- ☐ Write a song
- ☐ Pose for a photographer

Go on to the next block of activities.

(For later: Total number of check marks for this block: ⊕ = **your A total**

Which of these activities would you like doing?
(Check as many as you want.)

- ☐ Teach an individual an exercise routine
- ☐ Give CPR to someone who has stopped breathing
- ☐ Teach an elementary school class
- ☐ Supervise the activities of children at a camp
- ☐ Perform rehabilitation therapy
- ☐ Help elderly people with their daily activities
- ☐ Teach disabled people work and living skills
- ☐ Help people who have problems with drugs or alcohol
- ☐ Help families care for ill relatives
- ☐ Plan exercises for disabled patients
- ☐ Assist doctors in treating patients
- ☐ Teach children how to play sports
- ☐ Help conduct a group therapy session
- ☐ Organize activities at a recreational facility
- ☐ Counsel people who have a life-threatening illness

Go on to the next block of activities.

(For later: Total number of check marks for this block: ⟨⟩ = **your S total**

Which of these activities would you like doing?
(Check as many as you want.)

- ☑ Buy and sell stocks and bonds
- ☐ Sell candy and popcorn at sports events
- ☑ Manage a department within a large company
- ☑ Start your own business
- ☐ Represent a client in a lawsuit
- ☑ Be responsible for the operation of a company
- ☐ Sell automobiles
- ☐ Manage a retail store
- ☐ Operate a beauty salon or barber shop
- ☑ Sell houses
- ☑ Negotiate business contracts
- ☐ Market a new line of clothing
- ☐ Sell merchandise at a department store
- ☐ Manage a clothing store
- ☐ Sell computer equipment in a store

Go on to the next block of activities.

(For later: Total number of check marks for this block: ⟨6⟩ = **your E total**

Which of these activities would you like doing? (Check as many as you want.)

- ☐ Develop a spreadsheet using computer software
- ☑ Keep accounts payable/receivable for an office
- ☐ Transfer funds between banks using a computer
- ☐ Use a word processor to edit and format documents
- ☐ Direct or transfer phone calls for a large organization
- ☑ Compute and record statistical and other numerical data

35

- ☐ Take notes during a meeting
- ☐ Calculate the wages of employees
- ☐ Record information from customers applying for charge accounts
- ☐ Keep inventory records
- ☐ Stamp, sort, and distribute mail for an organization
- ☐ Proofread records or forms
- ☐ Schedule conferences for an organization
- ☐ Organize and schedule office meetings
- ☐ Keep shipping and receiving records

(For later: Total number of check marks for this block: 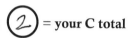 = **your C total**

NOW COUNT. Go back, count the check marks in each block of activities, and write the total at the bottom of each block.

Now, copy the total from each block to the table below.

TOTAL		PERSONALITY TYPE
For **R**	3	Realistic
For **I**	3	Investigative
For **A**	4	Artistic
For **S**	0	Social
For **E**	6	Enterprising
For **C**	2	Conventional

Which total has the highest number? Use that to identify your *primary personality type* in the right-hand column. Circle it.

Is there another total (maybe two) with a score that comes close to your highest number? Use these close seconds to identify one or two *secondary personality types* in the right-hand column. Underline these.

In the following table, find majors that are good matches for your primary personality type—and perhaps one or two secondary personality types. If you cannot find many majors that match the primary type, look under a secondary type. For example, let's say you are Artistic-Enterprising (primary is Artistic, secondary is Enterprising). You might look at Artistic majors and also at Enterprising majors, especially Enterprising-Artistic majors. You might consider some other majors with Artistic as their secondary type.

But what if you can't find an exact match for your personality profile, or you feel your options are too limited? People use various ways to accommodate the diverse aspects of their personality. Some use their free time in hobbies that engage interests they don't use on the job. Some find a niche job that fits their personality profile better than what is typical for their occupation.

Understand that the matches in the table are based on career paths that are typical for the majors. But some people plan for a career path that is not typical. For example, the Area Studies major is characterized as Social-Investigative-Artistic because the typical career path is to go into college teaching. However, someone with an Enterprising-Investigative profile and the goal of working in international business might major in Asian Studies (a specialization within Area Studies) in order to gain a deep understanding of Asian languages and culture. This person might be able to learn the business aspects of the career by completing a minor in a business field, by getting a master's degree in business administration (MBA), or even through on-the-job training. Or, for another example, a person with a Social-Investigative profile might major in a science (Investigative) for the bachelor's degree and then get a master's in education (Social), with the goal of becoming a science teacher.

So, in the following table, don't limit yourself to majors that exactly match your personality profile.

PERSONALITY TYPE(S)	MAJORS
Realistic	
Realistic-Enterprising-Conventional	Criminal Justice
Investigative	
Investigative-Realistic-Enterprising	Civil Engineering; Electrical Engineering; Mechanical Engineering
Investigative-Realistic-Conventional	Medical Technology
Investigative-Social-Realistic	Pre-Professional Health
Investigative-Enterprising	Geology
Investigative-Enterprising-Realistic	Aeronautical/Aerospace Engineering; Environmental Science
Investigative-Conventional-Realistic	Computer Engineering; Computer Science
Investigative-Conventional-Enterprising	Management Information Systems; Statistics
Artistic	
Artistic-Realistic	Studio Art
Artistic-Realistic-Social	Dance
Artistic-Enterprising	Journalism
Artistic-Enterprising-Realistic	Graphic Design

PERSONALITY TYPE(S)	MAJORS
Social	
Social	Business Education; Technology Education
Social-Investigative	Nursing (RN Training)
Social-Investigative-Artistic	Area Studies
Social-Artistic	Early Childhood Education; Family and Consumer Sciences Education; Modern Foreign Language; Special Education
Social-Artistic-Investigative	Philosophy
Social-Artistic-Enterprising	Biology; Chemistry; English; Mathematics; Physical Education; Physics; Secondary Education
Social-Artistic-Conventional	Elementary Education
Social-Enterprising	Social Work
Social-Enterprising-Artistic	Religious Studies
Enterprising	
Enterprising-Realistic-Conventional	Agricultural Business; Agronomy
Enterprising-Investigative	Agricultural Engineering; Architecture
Enterprising-Investigative-Realistic	Bioengineering; Chemical Engineering; Landscape Architecture; Metallurgical Engineering; Petroleum Engineering
Enterprising-Investigative-Conventional	Industrial Engineering

PERSONALITY TYPE(S)	MAJORS
Enterprising-Artistic	Communication; Theater Arts
Enterprising-Artistic-Social	Public Relations
Enterprising-Social-Conventional	History
Enterprising-Conventional	Business Management and Administration; Economics; Finance; Political Science; Psychology; Risk Management and Insurance; Sociology
Enterprising-Conventional-Investigative	Marketing
Enterprising-Conventional-Social	Health Facilities Administration; Hospitality Management; Human Resources Management
Conventional	
Conventional-Realistic-Investigative	Art History
Conventional-Enterprising	Accounting
Conventional-Enterprising-Investigative	Actuarial Science

Now, in the following box, write the names of majors that align well with aspects of your personality. Also, write in the names of any other majors that you think might be interesting.

KEY POINTS OF CHAPTER 2

> Personality types can be useful for summarizing factors that contribute to satisfaction and success in a college major and career.

> It can be helpful to consider not only your primary personality type, but also one or two secondary types.

> People sometimes accommodate a diverse personality profile by combining a major with a minor, a graduate degree, or an atypical career path.

CHAPTER 3

WHICH MAJORS USE MY STRONGEST SKILLS?

Like most people, you probably expect that college will give you the skills that you need to enter a career. But you're not a blank slate. You already have many skills, and in fact college will build on these skills. As a result, you're likely to be more successful in college majors that build on skills you already have.

This chapter will help you take stock of your work-related skills and will identify the majors that can take these skills to higher levels.

Following is a simple exercise that asks you to estimate your ability in nine specific skills. Some people find it hard to evaluate their skills, but just do the best you can.

1. READING COMPREHENSION

Definition: Understanding written sentences and paragraphs in work-related documents.

Examples of how you may have used this skill:

❭ Making inferences from what you've read.
❭ Relating background knowledge to something you're reading.

> Finding the main idea, important facts, and supporting details in something you're reading.

> Another good indicator, although it's not work-related, is your verbal score on a college admissions test.

Your skill at **Reading Comprehension**: Low, Medium, High (circle one)

High

2. FINANCIAL MANAGEMENT

Definition: Determining how money will be spent to get the work done and accounting for these expenditures.

Examples of how you may have used this skill:

> Balancing a checkbook.
> Preparing a budget.
> Comparing prices from multiple vendors.
> Listing income and expenses for an organization.

Your skill at **Financial Management**: Low, Medium, High (circle one)

L

3. MATHEMATICS

Definition: Using mathematics to solve problems: calculating; estimating; constructing mathematical models.

Examples of how you may have used this skill:

> Multiplying measurements to scale up a recipe.
> Computing sports statistics.
> Estimating how many cans of paint are needed to cover a house.

Your skill at **Mathematics**: Low, Medium, High (circle one)

M

4. SCIENCE

Definition: Using scientific rules and methods to solve problems: observing phenomena; proposing a hypothesis; making a prediction; designing and conducting experiments to test the prediction; constructing theories.

Examples of how you may have used this skill:

) Observing and studying the moon and stars.
) Experimenting to test a hypothesis about what caused a product to fail.
) Systematically altering your diet or exercise routine and testing the effects on your well-being.

Your skill at **Science**: Low, Medium, High (circle one)

5. SERVICE ORIENTATION

Definition: Actively looking for ways to help people.

Examples of how you may have used this skill:

) Taking care of sick relatives or friends.
) Teaching a skill to someone else.
) Doing volunteer work that helps other people.

Your skill at **Service Orientation**: Low, Medium, High (circle one)

6. EQUIPMENT MAINTENANCE

Definition: Performing routine maintenance and determining when and what kind of maintenance is needed.

Examples of how you may have used this skill:

) Changing a part on a plumbing fixture or vehicle.
) Running a diagnostic program on a computer.

How good is your skill at **Equipment Maintenance**? Low, Medium, High (circle one)

7. INSTALLATION

Definition: Installing equipment, machines, wiring, or programs to meet specifications.

Examples of how you may have used this skill:

❯ Loading an upgraded operating system onto a computer.

❯ Hooking up and setting up a digital video recorder.

❯ Installing an optional feature in a car.

Your skill at **Installation**: Low, Medium, High (circle one)

8. COMPUTER PROGRAMMING

Definition: Writing computer programs for various purposes—structuring the algorithm for the task at hand; organizing data storage; determining methods of input and output; choosing the right commands and syntax; correcting errors.

Examples of how you may have used this skill:

❯ Creating and modifying a macro in a word-processing program to accomplish a complex task.

❯ Writing a computer program to solve a math problem.

Your skill at **Computer Programming**: Low, Medium, High (circle one)

9. LEARNING STRATEGIES

Definition: Using multiple approaches when learning or teaching new things.

Examples of how you may have used this skill:

❭ Combining Web searches and phone calls to learn where to buy a particular product locally.
❭ Reading articles and getting input from family to learn the best way to defuse a conflict with a friend.

Your skill at **Learning Strategies:** Low, Medium, High (circle one)

LINKING YOUR SKILLS TO COLLEGE MAJORS

The previous skills are *specialized* skills. Now, it's time to match them to the generic skills that can be linked to college majors.

How does this matching work? Statistical analysis of skills in the workplace shows that specialized skills occur in clusters. That is, if a workplace demands one specialized skill, the odds are extremely high that there's also a need for certain related skills. For example, workplaces that demand skill at Reading Comprehension overwhelmingly demand skill at three additional skills: Active Listening, Speaking, and Writing. For a cluster like this, it is convenient to use a generic skill title (in this example, Communication) as an umbrella term for the whole cluster of skills.

Look at your responses to the previous checklist. In the left column of the following table, find the specific skills for which you rated your level **High**. Then, in the right column of the table, circle the generic skills that match them. (In some cases, the titles are the same in both columns.)

SPECIFIC SKILL FROM CHECKLIST	GENERIC SKILL
Reading Comprehension	Communication
Management of Financial Resources	Management
Mathematics	Mathematics
Science	Science

SPECIFIC SKILL FROM CHECKLIST	GENERIC SKILL
Service Orientation	Social
Equipment Maintenance	Equipment Use/Maintenance
Installation	Installation
Computer Programming	Technology/Programming
Learning Strategies	Thought-Processing

(If you are curious about which *other* specific skills are related to each of these generic skills, look in the appendix.)

Now, look at the college majors that are linked to each of your top generic skills. Underline the names of any majors that are linked to **more than one** of your high-level skills. Also underline the names of any other majors that you think might be interesting.

GENERIC SKILL	COLLEGE MAJORS
Communication	Accounting; Actuarial Science; Area Studies; Art History; Biology; Business Education; Chemistry; Communication; Criminal Justice; Early Childhood Education; Elementary Education; English; Family and Consumer Sciences Education; Geology; Human Resources Management; Journalism; Mathematics; Modern Foreign Language; Nursing (RN Training); Philosophy; Physical Education; Physics; Pre-Professional Health; Public Relations; Religious Studies; Risk Management and Insurance; Secondary Education; Special Education; Technology Education; Theater Arts

GENERIC SKILL	COLLEGE MAJORS
Equipment Use/ Maintenance	Agricultural Business; Agronomy; Hospitality Management; Medical Technology
Installation	Computer Engineering; Computer Science; Studio Art
Management	Agricultural Business; Agricultural Engineering; Agronomy; Architecture; Art History; Bioengineering; Business Education; Business Management and Administration; Chemical Engineering; Civil Engineering; Criminal Justice; Economics; Finance; Graphic Design; Health Facilities Administration; History; Hospitality Management; Industrial Engineering; Landscape Architecture; Marketing; Metallurgical Engineering; Petroleum Engineering; Political Science; Psychology; Public Relations; Religious Studies; Sociology; Studio Art; Technology Education; Theater Arts
Mathematics	Accounting; Actuarial Science; Aeronautical/ Aerospace Engineering; Agricultural Engineering; Architecture; Bioengineering; Chemical Engineering; Civil Engineering; Computer Engineering; Computer Science; Electrical Engineering; Environmental Science; Geology; Industrial Engineering; Landscape Architecture; Marketing; Mechanical Engineering; Medical Technology; Metallurgical Engineering; Petroleum Engineering; Risk Management and Insurance; Statistics

GENERIC SKILL	COLLEGE MAJORS
Science	Aeronautical/Aerospace Engineering; Agricultural Business; Agricultural Engineering; Agronomy; Architecture; Area Studies; Bioengineering; Chemical Engineering; Chemistry; Civil Engineering; Electrical Engineering; Environmental Science; Geology; Health Facilities Administration; Landscape Architecture; Management Information Systems; Mechanical Engineering; Medical Technology; Metallurgical Engineering; Nursing (RN Training); Petroleum Engineering; Philosophy; Pre-Professional Health; Social Work; Statistics
Social	Biology; Business Education; Business Management and Administration; Communication; Criminal Justice; Dance; Early Childhood Education; Economics; Elementary Education; English; Family and Consumer Sciences Education; Finance; History; Hospitality Management; Human Resources Management; Journalism; Mathematics; Modern Foreign Language; Nursing (RN Training); Physical Education; Physics; Political Science; Psychology; Public Relations; Religious Studies; Risk Management and Insurance; Secondary Education; Sociology; Special Education; Technology Education; Theater Arts

GENERIC SKILL	COLLEGE MAJORS
Technology/ Programming	Aeronautical/Aerospace Engineering; Computer Engineering; Computer Science; Dance; Electrical Engineering; Graphic Design; Industrial Engineering; Management Information Systems; Mechanical Engineering; Studio Art
Thought-Processing	Accounting; Actuarial Science; Area Studies; Art History; Biology; Business Management and Administration; Chemistry; Communication; Dance; Early Childhood Education; Economics; Elementary Education; English; Environmental Science; Family and Consumer Sciences Education; Finance; Graphic Design; Health Facilities Administration; History; Human Resources Management; Journalism; Management Information Systems; Marketing; Mathematics; Modern Foreign Language; Philosophy; Physical Education; Physics; Political Science; Pre-Professional Health; Psychology; Secondary Education; Sociology; Special Education; Statistics

Now, write the underlined majors in this box.

```
┌────────────────────────────────────────────┐
│                                            │
├────────────────────────────────────────────┤
│                                            │
├────────────────────────────────────────────┤
│                                            │
├────────────────────────────────────────────┤
│                                            │
├────────────────────────────────────────────┤
│                                            │
├────────────────────────────────────────────┤
│                                            │
├────────────────────────────────────────────┤
│                                            │
├────────────────────────────────────────────┤
│                                            │
├────────────────────────────────────────────┤
│                                            │
├────────────────────────────────────────────┤
│                                            │
├────────────────────────────────────────────┤
│                                            │
├────────────────────────────────────────────┤
│                                            │
├────────────────────────────────────────────┤
│                                            │
├────────────────────────────────────────────┤
│                                            │
└────────────────────────────────────────────┘
```

KEY POINTS OF CHAPTER 3

❭ College prepares you for a career by building on skills that you already have.

❭ Therefore, you should look for majors that are linked to workplace skills that you are good at.

❭ Your command of one detailed skill usually can predict your command of several related skills.

CHAPTER 4

WHICH MAJORS ARE CONSISTENT WITH MY EXPERIENCES IN HIGH SCHOOL?

Again and again, research studies have shown that your performance in high school is the single best predictor of your success in college. That's why it's important for you to consider your outstanding high school courses when you choose a college major.

Think about the courses that gave you enjoyment and good grades. Now, on the following list, choose 3 courses that you feel very good about.

Algebra (check Math instead)
Applied Communications (check Public Speaking instead)
☐ Art
☑ Biology
Calculus (check Math instead)
☐ Chemistry
☐ Computer Science
☐ Dance
☐ English

☑ Foreign Language
  Geography (check Social Science instead)
  Geometry (check Math instead)
  History (check Social Science instead)
☐ Home Economics
☐ Industrial Arts
☐ Keyboarding
  Literature (check English instead)
☑ Math
☐ Mechanical Drawing
☐ Music
☐ Office Computer Applications
☐ Photography
☐ Physics
  Pre-Calculus (check Math instead)
☐ Public Speaking
☐ Science
☐ Social Science
  Trigonometry (check Math instead)

In the following table, high school courses are linked to college majors that cover similar subject matter.

HIGH SCHOOL COURSE	COLLEGE MAJORS
Art	Architecture; Art History; Early Childhood Education; Elementary Education; Graphic Design; Journalism; Landscape Architecture; Public Relations; Secondary Education; Studio Art.

HIGH SCHOOL COURSE	COLLEGE MAJORS
Biology	Agricultural Business; Agricultural Engineering; Agronomy; Bioengineering; Biology; Dance; Environmental Science; Health Facilities Administration; Landscape Architecture; Medical Technology; Nursing (RN Training); Pre-Professional Health; Psychology; Social Work
Chemistry	Agricultural Business; Agricultural Engineering; Agronomy; Bioengineering; Biology; Chemical Engineering; Chemistry; Computer Science; Environmental Science; Geology; Health Facilities Administration; Mechanical Engineering; Medical Technology; Metallurgical Engineering; Nursing (RN Training); Petroleum Engineering; Physics; Pre-Professional Health; Secondary Education; Technology Education.
Computer Science	Accounting; Actuarial Science; Aeronautical/Aerospace Engineering; Agricultural Business; Agricultural Engineering; Agronomy; Bioengineering; Biology; Business Education; Business Management and Administration; Chemical Engineering; Chemistry; Civil Engineering; Computer Engineering; Computer Science; Electrical Engineering; Environmental Science; Geology; Graphic Design; Industrial Engineering; Landscape Architecture; Management Information Systems; Mathematics; Mechanical Engineering; Medical Technology; Metallurgical Engineering; Petroleum Engineering; Physics; Risk Management and Insurance; Statistics; Technology Education.

HIGH SCHOOL COURSE	COLLEGE MAJORS
Dance	Dance; Physical Education.
English	Area Studies; Art History; Communication; Computer Science; Economics; Early Childhood Education; Elementary Education; English; Graphic Design; Health Facilities Administration; History; Journalism; Medical Technology; Nursing (RN Training); Political Science; Pre-Professional Health; Psychology; Public Relations; Religious Studies; Secondary Education; Social Work; Sociology.
Foreign Language	Area Studies; Art History; Communication; Dance; Elementary Education; English; History; Journalism; Modern Foreign Language; Philosophy; Religious Studies; Secondary Education; Social Work; Sociology; Studio Art; Theater Arts.
Home Economics	Business Education; Family and Consumer Sciences Education; Secondary Education.
Industrial Arts	Technology Education.
Keyboarding	Business Education; Technology Education.

HIGH SCHOOL COURSE	COLLEGE MAJORS
Math	Accounting; Actuarial Science; Aeronautical/ Aerospace Engineering; Agricultural Engineering; Architecture; Bioengineering; Biology; Business Education; Business Management and Administration; Chemical Engineering; Chemistry; Civil Engineering; Computer Engineering; Computer Science; Economics; Electrical Engineering; Family and Consumer Sciences Education; Finance; Geology; Graphic Design; Health Facilities Administration; Hospitality Management; Human Resources Management; Industrial Engineering; Landscape Architecture; Management Information Systems; Marketing; Mathematics; Mechanical Engineering; Metallurgical Engineering; Petroleum Engineering; Physics; Pre-Professional Health; Risk Management and Insurance; Secondary Education; Statistics; Technology Education.
Mechanical Drawing	Graphic Design; Technology Education.
Music	Dance; Early Childhood Education; Elementary Education; Secondary Education.
Office Computer Applications	Business Education; Health Facilities Administration; Management Information Systems; Technology Education.
Photography	Graphic Design; Technology Education.

HIGH SCHOOL COURSE	COLLEGE MAJORS
Physics	Aeronautical/Aerospace Engineering; Agricultural Engineering; Architecture; Bioengineering; Biology; Chemical Engineering; Chemistry; Civil Engineering; Computer Engineering; Computer Science; Electrical Engineering; Geology; Landscape Architecture; Mathematics; Mechanical Engineering; Medical Technology; Metallurgical Engineering; Petroleum Engineering; Physics; Pre-Professional Health; Secondary Education; Statistics; Technology Education.
Public Speaking	Agronomy; Business Education; Business Management and Administration; Communication; Criminal Justice; Early Childhood Education; Elementary Education; English; Environmental Science; Family and Consumer Sciences Education; Graphic Design; Health Facilities Administration; Journalism; Modern Foreign Language; Nursing (RN Training); Physical Education; Pre-Professional Health; Public Relations; Religious Studies; Secondary Education; Social Work; Special Education; Technology Education; Theater Arts.

HIGH SCHOOL COURSE	COLLEGE MAJORS
Science	Aeronautical/Aerospace Engineering; Agricultural Business; Agricultural Engineering; Agronomy; Architecture; Bioengineering; Biology; Business Management and Administration; Chemical Engineering; Chemistry; Civil Engineering; Computer Engineering; Elementary Education; Electrical Engineering; Computer Science; Environmental Science; Geology; Industrial Engineering; Mechanical Engineering; Medical Technology; Metallurgical Engineering; Nursing (RN Training); Petroleum Engineering; Physics; Pre-Professional Health; Secondary Education; Technology Education.
Social Science	Area Studies; Art History; Communication; Criminal Justice; Economics; Elementary Education; English; Environmental Science; Family and Consumer Sciences Education; Health Facilities Administration; History; Human Resources Management; Journalism; Marketing; Modern Foreign Language; Philosophy; Political Science; Psychology; Public Relations; Religious Studies; Secondary Education; Social Work; Sociology; Studio Art.

Look over the college majors that are linked to your favorite high school courses. Underline the names of any majors that linked to more than one of your favorite courses. Also underline the names of any other majors that you think might be interesting.

Now, write the underlined majors in the box below.

KEY POINTS OF CHAPTER 4

❯ Your high school grades are the single best predictors of your success in college.

❯ High school classes that you enjoyed can point toward college majors that you might also enjoy.

CHAPTER 5

WHAT ARE MY LISTS TELLING ME?

In the three previous chapters, you did exercises that resulted in lists of college majors that you may want to explore. If you have lots of time, you can investigate all of these majors. But if you want to save time, you now should look for patterns in your lists so you can assemble a small **Hot List**.

Which of the following statements applies best to your lists in the three previous chapters?

)   *Certain majors appear in all three lists.* Great! Clearly, these are the majors that you should investigate in detail. Write these majors in the Hot List.

)   *Certain majors appear in two out of the three lists.* This is a strong indication. Now, ask yourself how confident you feel about the way you answered each exercise. For example, do have a clearer notion of your high school performance than you do of your personality type? You may want to give greater weight to the majors identified by the two exercises that you feel most confident about. With this in mind, choose the majors to write in the Hot List.

)   *I don't see any pattern. No major (or almost none) appears in more than one list.* You'll need to decide which exercise you trust the most. Your performance in high school is usually the best single predictor of your success in college, but possibly you feel more confident about the majors that align with your personality or your skills. Use the list generated by one exercise to populate the Hot List. If a few majors from the other two exercises intrigue you, include them, too.

Once you have filled out your Hot List, you're ready to start reading about these majors in chapter 6. Then you'll look at the facts about related careers in chapter 7. As you read these descriptions and form impressions—positive or negative—use the Hot List as a score card:

❯ Use stars, checkmarks, or underlines to indicate the majors that look like the hottest of the hot. Cross out any majors that look as if they would not suit you.

❯ Next to each major that appeals to you, write the names of any related occupations that seem to deserve a closer look.

MY HOT LIST

software
engineering
business &
film / multi-media

KEY POINTS OF CHAPTER 5

❯ If some majors are identified by all three exercises, they probably deserve further exploration.

❯ If you can't find majors that are consistent with all three exercises, focus on the results of the one or two exercises that you feel most confident about.

CHAPTER 6

DESCRIPTIONS OF COLLEGE MAJORS

In this chapter, you'll find descriptions of 61 popular college majors. Although you'll probably want to concentrate on the majors from your Hot List, you may also want to browse other majors that look intriguing. You may be pleasantly surprised by what you find when you wander around in this chapter.

Majors in this chapter are ordered alphabetically by title, but a few (the majors that prepare for careers in business management, education, and engineering) are grouped together because they share certain core courses. If you look for a major under an alternate name, a cross-reference will steer you toward the title and page where you can find the description.

The facts for each major are arranged so you can easily form a first impression of what the major involves and where it leads to. For any major that interests you, turn to chapter 7 and read the facts about related occupations.

Understand that chapters 6 and 7 are only first stages in a thorough exploration of a major. I know you may be pressed for time, but any commitment you make now should be considered tentative. Follow through with some of the ideas in chapter 8 about how to confirm your choice.

Here's what you'll find for each major:

> **Title and definition.** The definition is derived from the Classification of Instructional Programs (CIP), a system developed by the U.S. Department of Education to catalog every major. In some cases, the description is followed by "Also Known As," plus the names of one or more alternative titles that are commonly used in colleges.

> **Specializations in the Major.** These are also known as concentrations or tracks. Often they are based on the different careers that graduates go into. Your college may offer more, fewer, or different specializations than the ones listed here.

> **Courses Studied in College.** These are the courses that typically are required for the major, listed roughly in the order in which you would take them. You may study some of these subjects for more than one semester. Understand that this list is a generalization, because each college has its own unique requirements for the major. Often you have the ability to choose from several courses related to the major. For example, the catalog might say, "You must take 2 of the following 5 advanced courses." Also, this list does not include requirements that are not related to the particular major but are expected of all degree candidates.

> **Usual High School Prerequisites.** These are courses that are considered good preparation for the major. You may need to study some of them for more than one year. If you did not take one these courses in high school, you may be able to prepare for the major by taking a similar course in your first year or two of college.

> **Related Occupations.** These are occupations that are considered typical career outcomes of the major, and the major may be designed to prepare you for one or more of these careers. (The occupations are described in chapter 7, where they are ordered alphabetically.) Understand that sometimes an additional degree may be required to enter one of these occupations. Also keep in mind that with an additional degree, it may be possible to enter some career not listed here. For example, if your bachelor's degree is not in a business subject, a master's in business administration (MBA) may open the door to a business career. In addition, a doctoral degree in almost any

field may be your route to teaching that subject in college or doing original research.

❭ **Career Paths.** This paragraph gives additional information about the typical career outcomes of the major. It often indicates which industries employ graduates, how graduates may advance in their careers, and what career specializations currently offer the best job prospects.

ACCOUNTING

see Business Majors, p. 73.

ACTUARIAL SCIENCE

Focuses on the mathematical and statistical analysis of risk, and their applications to insurance and other business management problems. Includes instruction in forecasting theory, quantitative and non-quantitative risk measurement methodologies, development of risk tables, secondary data analysis, and computer-assisted research methods. **Also Known As:** Actuarial Studies.

Specializations in the Major: Insurance; investment.

Courses Studied in College: Business writing; calculus; advanced calculus; introduction to marketing; introduction to computer science; introduction to probability; introduction to actuarial mathematics; mathematical statistics; applied regression; actuarial models; introduction to accounting; principles of microeconomics; principles of macroeconomics; financial management; investment analysis. **Usual High School Prerequisites:** English; algebra; geometry; trigonometry; science; pre-calculus; calculus; computer science.

Related Occupations: Actuaries (p. 148); Insurance Underwriters (p. 210).

Career Paths: Actuaries analyze the financial costs of risk and uncertainty. They use mathematics, statistics, and financial theory to assess the risk that an event will occur and they help businesses and clients develop policies that minimize the cost of that risk. They must have a strong background in mathematics, statistics, and business. Actuaries need a bachelor's degree and must pass a series of exams to become certified professionals. Many employers expect students to have passed at least one of the initial actuary exams needed for professional certification before graduation. Most entry-level actuaries start out as trainees. Advancement depends largely on job performance and the number of actuarial exams passed. Strong competition for jobs is expected. Actuaries make up a small occupation, and the relatively high pay and comfortable working conditions make being an actuary a desirable career. Students who have passed at least two actuarial exams and have had an internship while in college should have the best job prospects for entry-level positions.

AERONAUTICAL/AEROSPACE ENGINEERING

see Engineering Majors, p. 98.

AFRICAN AMERICAN STUDIES

see Area Studies, p. 68.

AGRICULTURAL BUSINESS

Focuses on modern business and economic principles involved in the organization, operation, and management of agricultural enterprises. **Also Known As:** Agribusiness.

Specializations in the Major: Agricultural economics; agricultural finance; agricultural marketing and sales; computer applications and data management; farm and rural policy; farm business management.

Courses Studied in College: English composition; oral communication; business math; general biology; introduction to economics; introduction to accounting; introduction to agricultural economics and business; farm/ranch management; computer applications in agriculture; legal environment of agriculture; statistics for business and social sciences; microeconomic theory; macroeconomic theory; natural resource economics; agribusiness financial management; introduction to marketing; marketing and pricing agricultural products; technical writing; agricultural policy and trade; quantitative methods in agricultural business. **Usual High School Prerequisites:** English; algebra; geometry; trigonometry; biology; chemistry; computer science.

Related Occupations: Farmers, Ranchers, and Other Agricultural Managers (p. 190).

Career Paths: Like other major industries, agriculture offers many different business careers. Besides production (that is, farming), graduates of this program may work in finance, making loans to farm businesses; marketing, finding customers for agricultural products; government or nonprofits, researching or setting policies for land development and resource management; or management of the many kinds of businesses that supply farmers or buy farm output. Those who have specialized in agricultural economics may work in commodities trading. A graduate degree is useful for teaching or research positions.

AGRICULTURAL ENGINEERING

see Engineering Majors, p. 99.

AGRONOMY

Focuses on the chemical, physical, and biological relationships of crops and the soils nurturing them. Includes instruction in the growth and behavior of agricultural crops, the development of new plant varieties, and the scientific management of soils and nutrients for maximum plant nutrition, health, and productivity.

Specializations in the Major: Agricultural meteorology; plant breeding and genetics; plant physiology and biochemistry; soil and crop management; turfgrass management; water resources planning and management; weed science.

Courses Studied in College: College algebra; statistics; general biology; general chemistry; genetics; introduction to agricultural economics and business; introduction to soil science; computer applications in agriculture; plant pathology; crop production; soil fertility, plant nutrition and fertilizers; general entomology; weed control. **Usual High School Prerequisites:** Biology; chemistry; algebra; geometry; trigonometry; computer science; English; public speaking.

Related Occupations: Farmers, Ranchers, and Other Agricultural Managers (p. 190); First-Line Supervisors of Farming, Fishing, and Forestry Workers (p. 197); Soil and Plant Scientists (p. 255).

Career Paths: For agronomists and crop scientists, most job growth over the next 10 years will be in private industry. Bachelor's degree holders may work in applied research or as agricultural products inspectors. A graduate degree is usually needed to do the basic research—for example, in genomics and agricultural sustainability—that is expected to grow in coming years. A graduate degree is also needed to teach in college.

AMERICAN STUDIES

see Area Studies, p. 68.

ANTHROPOLOGY

see Sociology, p.138.

ARCHITECTURE

Prepares individuals for the independent professional practice of architecture and to conduct research in various aspects of the field. Includes instruction in architectural design, history, and theory; building structures and environmental systems; project and site planning; construction; professional responsibilities and standards; and related cultural, social, economic, and environmental issues.

Specializations in the Major: Architectural engineering; building information modeling; building technology/environmental systems design; history; preservation; sustainability; theory and criticism; urban studies.

Courses Studied in College: English composition; basic drawing; calculus; general physics; history of architecture; structures; architectural technology; construction materials and methods; architectural graphics; architectural design; seminar (reporting on research). **Usual High School Prerequisites:** English; algebra; geometry; trigonometry; pre-calculus; calculus; physics; computer science; art.

Related Occupations: Architects, Except Landscape and Naval (p. 152); Architectural and Engineering Managers (p. 153); Construction Managers (p. 178).

Career Paths: Although the five-year bachelor's program is the most common entry route for architects, some enter via a master's program that may take one to five years, depending on previous course work in architectural subjects. All state architectural registration boards require architecture graduates to complete a lengthy paid internship—most require at least three years of experience—before they may sit for the Architect Registration Exam. Strong competition for internships and jobs in the field is expected, especially at the most prestigious architectural firms. Employment of architects is strongly tied to the activity of the construction industry. Therefore, these workers may experience periods of unemployment when there is a slowdown in requests for new projects or when the overall level of construction falls.

AREA STUDIES

Focuses on the history, society, politics, culture, and economics of a nation, a geographical region, an ethnic group, or another human group. **Also Known As:** African American Studies; American Studies; Asian Studies; Gender Studies; Latin American Studies; LGBT Studies; Peace Studies; Women's Studies.

Specializations in the Major: A region; an ethnicity; economics and trade; history and culture; language and literature; peace studies; women's studies.

Courses Studied in College: English composition; foreign language; introduction to study of specific area (e.g., women, African Americans, Latin America); literature and culture of area; history of area; global perspective on area; seminar (reporting on research). **Usual High School Prerequisites:** English; foreign language; history; literature; social science; algebra; geography.

Related Occupations: Area, Ethnic, and Cultural Studies Teachers, Postsecondary (p. 154).

Career Paths: Some of the more popular area studies are African American studies, American studies, and women's studies, but this kind of major may focus on some other region of the world (such as Latin American studies) or aspect of culture (such as urban studies). Students approach their area of interest using the methods of several disciplines, such as linguistics, literature, history, sociology, political science, and economic development. Usually you can emphasize whichever aspects interest you most. The knowledge and skills acquired in such a program can be useful for a career in a business, a nonprofit organization, or a government agency that targets one of these geographical regions or cultures. Some graduates get an additional degree and enter a career in law or college teaching.

ARABIC

see Modern Foreign Language, p. 124.

ART HISTORY

Focuses on the study of the historical development of art as social and intellectual phenomenon, the analysis of works of art, and art conservation. Includes instruction in the theory of art, art history research methods, connoisseurship, the preservation and conservation of works of art, and the study of specific periods, cultures, styles, and themes.

Specializations in the Major: A historical period; a particular artistic medium; a region of the world; criticism; museum studies.

Courses Studied in College: English composition; foreign language; studio art; art history—prehistoric to Renaissance or Renaissance to modern; non-Western art; seminar (reporting on research). **Usual High School Prerequisites:** English; art; foreign language; history; literature; social science.

Related Occupations: Archivists (p. 154); Curators (p. 181); Museum Technicians and Conservators (p. 227).

Career Paths: Graduates of art history programs with a bachelor's degree may work for museums, auction houses, or publishers. Work as a college teacher or as an art restorer usually requires a graduate degree. A graduate degree in museology may lead to work as a museum technician or curator. However, many employers feel that a thorough knowledge of the museum's specialty and museum work experience are more important than the degree. Particularly in small museums, curators may have administrative and managerial responsibilities, so courses in business administration, public relations, marketing, and fundraising are recommended.

ASIAN STUDIES

see Area Studies, p. 68.

BEHAVIORAL SCIENCE

see Psychology, p. 132.

BIOENGINEERING

see Engineering Majors, p. 100.

BIOLOGY

A general program of biology at the introductory, basic level or a program in biology or the biological sciences that is undifferentiated as to title or content. Includes instruction in general biology and programs covering a variety of biological specializations. **Also Known As:** Botany; Cell Biology; Genetics; Life Sciences; Microbiology; Zoology.

Specializations in the Major: Biochemistry; botany; cell biology; ecology; forensic science; genetics; microbiology; molecular biology; zoology.

Courses Studied in College: English composition; calculus; introduction to computer science; general chemistry; statistics; general biology; organic chemistry; genetics; general physics; cell biology; introduction to biochemistry; ecology and evolution; research methods. **Usual High School Prerequisites:** Algebra; English; biology; geometry; trigonometry; chemistry; physics; pre-calculus; calculus; computer science.

Related Occupations: Biological Scientists, All Other (p. 156); Life Scientists, All Other (p. 213); Natural Sciences Managers (p. 227); Secondary School Teachers, Except Special and Career/Technical Education (p. 251).

Career Paths: Many colleges offer majors that specialize in a field of life science such as botany, zoology, or biochemistry. A bachelor's degree in biology or in one of these subfields may lead to a career as a technician or entry-level researcher in a medical, pharmaceutical, or governmental regulatory setting, or as a sales representative in a technical field such as agriculture or pharmaceuticals. Good job opportunities are expected in these fields. Some grads get additional course work (perhaps a master's), plus supervised classroom experience, to qualify for a job teaching biology in high school or middle school. A graduate or professional degree can lead to a career as a researcher, college teacher, physician, dentist, veterinarian, or other health-care professional. The outlook in health care is generally very good, but the competition for admission to a postgraduate program can be intense.

BIOMEDICAL ENGINEERING

see Engineering Majors, p. 101.

BOTANY

see Biology, p. 71.

BUSINESS ADMINISTRATION

see Business Majors, p. 72.

BUSINESS EDUCATION

see Education Majors, p. 89.

BUSINESS MAJORS

BUSINESS MANAGEMENT (CORE)

For upper-division courses, see the following business specializations.

Lower-Division College Courses: English composition; business writing; introduction to psychology; principles of microeconomics; principles of macroeconomics; calculus for business and social sciences; statistics for business and social sciences; introduction to management information systems; introduction to accounting; legal environment of business; principles of management and organization; operations management; strategic management; business finance; introduction to marketing; organizational behavior; human resource management; international management; organizational theory. **Usual High School Prerequisites:** English; algebra; geometry; trigonometry; science; foreign language; computer science; public speaking.

ACCOUNTING (UPPER DIVISION)

Prepares individuals to practice the profession of accounting and to perform related business functions. Includes instruction in accounting principles and theory, financial accounting, managerial accounting, cost accounting, budget control, tax accounting, legal aspects of accounting, auditing, reporting procedures, statement analysis, planning and consulting, business information systems, accounting research methods, professional standards and ethics, and applications to specific for-profit, public, and non-profit organizations.

Specializations in the Major: Auditing; computer systems; cost; fiduciary; financial reporting; forensic; managerial; taxation.

For lower-division courses, see Business Management (Core), p. 72.

Upper-Division College Courses: Operations management; cost accounting; auditing; organizational behavior; federal income tax; advanced accounting. **Usual High School Prerequisites:** English; algebra; geometry; trigonometry; science; foreign language; computer science.

Related Occupations: Accountants and Auditors (p. 147); Budget Analysts (p. 159); Credit Analysts (p. 181); Financial Examiners (p. 192); Tax Examiners and Collectors, and Revenue Agents (p. 262).

Career Paths: Most accountant and auditor positions require at least a bachelor's degree in accounting or a related field. A few universities and colleges offer specialized programs, such as a bachelor's degree in internal auditing. In general, employment growth of accountants and auditors is expected to be closely tied to the health of the overall economy. Accountants and auditors who have earned professional recognition, especially as Certified Public Accountants (CPAs), should have the best prospects. Job applicants who have a master's degree in accounting or a master's degree in business with a concentration in accounting also may have an advantage. However, competition should be strong for jobs with the most prestigious accounting and business firms.

BUSINESS MANAGEMENT AND ADMINISTRATION (UPPER DIVISION)

Prepares individuals to plan, organize, direct, and control the functions and processes of a firm or organization. Includes instruction in management theory, human resources management and behavior, accounting and other quantitative methods, purchasing and logistics, organization and production, marketing, and business decision-making. **Also Known As:** Business Administration.

Specializations in the Major: E-commerce; international business; logistics; nonprofits; operations; projects; public administration; real estate; sales; technology entrepreneurship.

For lower-division courses, see Business Management (Core), p. 72.

Upper-Division College Courses: Business ethics; team-building and leadership; decision-making tools for managers. **Usual High School Prerequisites:** English; algebra; geometry; trigonometry; science; foreign language; computer science; public speaking.

Related Occupations: Administrative Services Managers (p. 149); Chief Executives (p. 161); Construction Managers (p. 178); Cost Estimators (p. 179); General and Operations Managers (p. 200); Industrial Production Managers (p. 205); Management Analysts (p. 215); Managers, All Other (p. 215); Sales Managers (p. 250); Social and Community Service Managers (p. 252); Training and Development Managers (p. 263); Transportation, Storage, and Distribution Managers (p. 264).

Career Paths: Graduates with a general degree in business may enter many specializations, such as marketing, finance, or human resource management. Some get entry-level work experience of some kind and then enter a master's of business administration program to learn more-specialized skills. Check the occupational descriptions in chapter 7 for the outlook for business specializations.

FINANCE (UPPER DIVISION)

Prepares individuals to plan, manage, and analyze the financial and monetary aspects and performance of business enterprises, banking institutions, or other organizations. Includes instruction in principles of accounting, financial instruments, capital planning, funds acquisition, asset and debt management, budgeting, financial analysis, and investments and portfolio management.

Specializations in the Major: Asset management; corporate; international; nonprofit; public; securities analysis.

For lower-division courses, see Business Management (Core), p. 72.

Upper-Division College Courses: Corporate finance; money and capital markets; investment analysis; international finance; financial accounting; risk management. **Usual High School Prerequisites:** English; algebra; geometry; trigonometry; science; foreign language; computer science.

Related Occupations: Budget Analysts (p. 159); Chief Executives (p. 161); Credit Analysts (p. 181); Financial Analysts (p. 192); Financial Managers (p. 193); Financial Specialists, All Other (p. 194); General and Operations Managers (p. 200); Loan Officers (p. 214); Personal Financial Advisors (p. 232).

Career Paths: Finance is a discipline that deals with how resources are allocated to corporations, institutions such as banks, and individuals. Financial professionals help all three kinds of entities to acquire funds and use them in ways that maximize their value. The workers use a combination of superior quantitative ability with effective communication skills. A bachelor's degree is good preparation for entry-level jobs. With an additional five or more years of experience, a job as a financial manager becomes a possibility. Because the jobs are often paid well, jobseekers can expect a fair amount of competition. But because the United States remains an international financial center, job opportunities should be good, except during times of financial downturn.

HOSPITALITY MANAGEMENT (UPPER DIVISION)

Prepares individuals to serve as general managers and directors of hospitality operations on a system-wide basis, including both travel arrangements and promotion and the provision of traveler facilities. Includes instruction in principles of operations in the travel and tourism, hotel and lodging facilities, food services, and recreation facilities industries; hospitality marketing strategies; hospitality planning; management and coordination of franchise and unit operations; business management; accounting and financial management; hospitality transportation and logistics; and hospitality industry policies and regulations. **Also Known As:** Hotel Management; Motel Management; Restaurant Management.

Specializations in the Major: Casinos; hotels/motels; hospitality marketing; resorts and theme parks; restaurants; spas.

For lower-division courses, see Business Management (Core), p. 72.

Upper-Division College Courses: Introduction to the hospitality industry; food and beverage production and management; food service and lodging operations; law for the hospitality industry; hospitality financial management; hospitality marketing; hospitality human resource management; hospitality technology applications; field experience/internship. **Usual High School Prerequisites:** English; algebra; geometry; trigonometry; science; foreign language; computer science; public speaking.

Related Occupations: Food Service Managers (p. 199); Lodging Managers (p. 214).

Career Paths: Many applicants for jobs in lodging management qualify by having a high school diploma and several years of experience working in a hotel. However, most large, full-service hotels require applicants to have a bachelor's degree. Hotels that provide fewer services generally accept applicants who have an associate's degree or certificate in hotel management or operations. For jobs in restaurant management, most applicants qualify with a high school diploma and long-term work experience in the food service industry as a cook, waiter or waitress, or counter attendant. However, some receive training at a community college, technical or vocational school, culinary school, or at a four-year college. Those seeking jobs at hotels with the highest level of guest services are expected to face strong competition, as these positions are highly sought after by people trained in hospitality management or administration. Applicants with a bachelor's degree in hospitality or hotel management are expected to have the best job opportunities, particularly at upscale and luxury hotels. Similarly, for restaurant management jobs, a combination of work experience in food service and a bachelor's degree in hospitality, restaurant, or food service management should give applicants an edge when competing for jobs at upscale restaurants.

HOTEL MANAGEMENT

see Hospitality Management (Upper Division), p. 76.

HUMAN RESOURCES MANAGEMENT (UPPER DIVISION)

Prepares individuals to manage the development of human capital in organizations, and to provide related services to individuals and groups. Includes instruction in personnel and organization policy, human resource dynamics and flows, labor relations, sex roles, civil rights, human resources law and regulations, motivation and compensation systems, work systems, career management, employee testing and assessment, recruitment and selection, managing employee and job training programs, and the management of human resources programs and operations. **Also Known As:** Personnel Management.

Specializations in the Major: Career management; compensation/ benefits; job analysis; labor relations; training.

For lower-division courses, see Business Management (Core), p. 72.

Upper-Division College Courses: Compensation and benefits administration; training and development; employment law; staffing organizations. **Usual High School Prerequisites:** English; algebra; geometry; trigonometry; science; foreign language; computer science; public speaking.

Related Occupations: Compensation and Benefits Managers (p. 169); Compensation, Benefits, and Job Analysis Specialists (p. 169); Human Resources Managers (p. 203); Human Resources Specialists (p. 203); Labor Relations Specialists (p. 212); Training and Development Managers (p. 263); Training and Development Specialists (p. 263).

Career Paths: Candidates for work in human resources management need a combination of education and several years of related work experience. Although a bachelor's degree is sufficient for most positions, some jobs require a master's degree. Candidates should have strong interpersonal skills. The HR Certification Institute and the International Foundation of Employee Benefit Plans are among many professional associations that offer a variety of certification programs. Although job opportunities are expected to vary based on the staffing needs of individual companies, very strong competition can be expected for most positions. Job opportunities should be best in companies that help other firms with some of their human resources functions. Candidates with certification or a master's degree—particularly those with a concentration in human resources management—should have the best job prospects. Those with a solid background in human resources programs, policies, and employment law should also have better job opportunities.

INSURANCE

see Risk Management and Insurance (Upper Division), p. 81.

MANAGEMENT INFORMATION SYSTEMS (UPPER DIVISION)

Prepares individuals to provide and manage data systems and related facilities for processing and retrieving internal business information; select systems and train personnel; and respond to external data requests. Includes instruction in cost and accounting information systems, management control systems, personnel information systems, data storage and security, business systems networking, report preparation, computer facilities and equipment operation and maintenance, operator supervision and training, and management information systems policy and planning. **Also Known As:** MIS.

Specializations in the Major: Accounting; analytics and business intelligence; database and Internet technologies; medical informatics; project management; security and disaster recovery.

For lower-division courses, see Business Management (Core), p. 72.

Upper-Division College Courses: Database management systems; systems analysis and design; business data communications; business application development; information system security. **Usual High School Prerequisites:** English; algebra; geometry; trigonometry; science; foreign language; computer science.

Related Occupations: Computer and Information Systems Managers (p. 170); Computer Programmers (p. 177).

Career Paths: Like other business majors, the MIS program gives students a firm grounding in economics, accounting, business law, finance, and marketing, as well as technical skills needed to work with computers. Students may specialize in MIS at either the bachelor's or master's level and may combine it with a degree in a related business field, such as accounting or finance, or in computer science. Some graduates work as network and computer systems administrators or database administrators in business settings. The job outlook is good.

MARKETING (UPPER DIVISION)

Prepares individuals to undertake and manage the process of developing consumer audiences and moving products from producers to consumers. Includes instruction in buyer behavior and dynamics, principles of marketing research, demand analysis, cost-volume and profit relationships, pricing theory, marketing campaign and strategic planning, market segments, advertising methods, sales operations and management, consumer relations, retailing, and applications to specific products and markets. **Also Known As:** Sales Management.

Specializations in the Major: Brand management; distribution management; franchise marketing; marketing management; marketing research; sales.

For lower-division courses, see Business Management (Core), p. 72.

Upper-Division College Courses: Marketing research methods; consumer behavior; marketing management; international marketing. **Usual High School Prerequisites:** English; algebra; geometry; trigonometry; science; foreign language; computer science.

Related Occupations: Advertising and Promotions Managers (p. 149); Market Research Analysts and Marketing Specialists (p. 218); Marketing Managers (p. 219); Sales Managers (p. 250).

Career Paths: Most market research analysts need at least a bachelor's degree. Strong math and analytical skills are essential. With work experience, a marketing management position becomes a possibility. Some market research analyst jobs require a master's degree. Several schools offer graduate programs in marketing research, but many analysts complete degrees in other fields, such as statistics and marketing, or earn a master's in business administration (MBA). A master's degree is often required for leadership positions or positions that perform more technical research. Completing an internship while in school is highly recommended. Overall job prospects for market research analysts are expected to be good. Rapid employment growth in most industries means good job opportunities should be available. Job prospects should be best for those with a master's degree in market research, marketing, statistics, or business administration. Candidates with only a bachelor's degree are expected to face strong competition for jobs. Those with a strong background in statistical and data analysis or related work experience will have better job opportunities than those without it.

MIS

see Management Information Systems (Upper Division), p. 79.

MOTEL MANAGEMENT

see Hospitality Management (Upper Division), p. 76.

PERSONNEL MANAGEMENT

see Human Resources Management (Upper Division), p. 77.

RESTAURANT MANAGEMENT

see Hospitality Management (Upper Division), p. 76.

RISK MANAGEMENT AND INSURANCE (UPPER DIVISION)

Prepares individuals to manage risk in organizational settings and provide insurance and risk-aversion services to businesses, individuals, and other organizations. Includes instruction in casualty insurance and general liability, property insurance, employee benefits, social and health insurance, loss adjustment, underwriting, risk theory, and pension planning. **Also Known As:** Insurance.

Specializations in the Major: Commercial risk management; financial planning; life and health; property and liability.

For lower-division courses, see Business Management (Core), p. 72.

Upper-Division College Courses: Property and liability insurance; life and health insurance; commercial risk management; legal aspects of insurance; employee benefits; insurer operations and policy. **Usual High School Prerequisites:** English; algebra; geometry; trigonometry; science; foreign language; computer science.

Related Occupations: Claims Adjusters, Examiners, and Investigators (p. 165); Insurance Appraisers, Auto Damage (p. 209); Insurance Sales Agents (p. 210); Insurance Underwriters (p. 210).

Career Paths: A bachelor's degree in insurance may lead to employment as an agent or broker; a corporate risk manager; a claims adjuster; an insurance underwriter; an estate planner; an insurance fraud investigator; or an actuary (with passage of at least one of the initial certification exams). Mergers and downsizing among agencies and brokerages, plus automation of some routine procedures, may limit the number of job openings. Jobseekers can expect a fair amount of competition in the finance industry because of the high pay in many careers. In insurance agencies, applicants with strong computer and communication skills should expect the best opportunities.

SALES MANAGEMENT

see Marketing (Upper Division), p. 80.

BUSINESS MANAGEMENT AND ADMINISTRATION

see Business Majors, p. 72.

CELL BIOLOGY

see Biology, p. 71.

CHEMICAL ENGINEERING

see Engineering Majors, p. 102.

CHEMISTRY

Focuses on the scientific study of the composition and behavior of matter, including its micro- and macrostructure, the processes of chemical change, and the theoretical description and laboratory simulation of these phenomena.

Specializations in the Major: Analytical; biochemistry; clinical; environmental; foods; forensic; geological/ocean; inorganic; materials; pharmaceutical; nuclear; organic; physical; polymers; quality control; research.

Courses Studied in College: English composition; calculus; introduction to computer science; general chemistry; organic chemistry; qualitative analysis; quantitative analysis; general physics; physical chemistry; inorganic chemistry; research methods; advanced laboratory in chemistry. **Usual High School Prerequisites:** English; algebra; geometry; trigonometry; pre-calculus; calculus; chemistry; physics; computer science.

Related Occupations: Chemists (p. 161); Natural Sciences Managers (p. 227); Secondary School Teachers, Except Special and Career/Technical Education (p. 251).

Career Paths: Chemistry is the science of matter and of the changes it undergoes. Chemists research the nature and properties of matter to develop new and improved products and to test the quality of manufactured goods. A bachelor's degree is usually required for entry to this field, but a master's or PhD is often needed for research or college teaching. Chemists with advanced degrees, particularly those with a PhD and work experience, are expected to experience better opportunities.

CHINESE

see Modern Foreign Language, p. 124.

CIVIL ENGINEERING

see Engineering Majors, p. 103.

CLINICAL LABORATORY SCIENCE

see Medical Technology, p. 123.

COMMUNICATION

Focuses on the comprehensive study of communication and can also span the study of mass communication/media studies, old and new media technologies, social and political applications, and speech communication and rhetoric. Includes instruction in interpersonal, group, organizational, and intercultural communication; theories of communication; critical thinking, argumentation, and persuasion; written communication; printed, electronic, and digital media; rhetorical tradition and criticism; media, society, and culture; consequences and effects of mass media; media social science and criticism; and quantitative and qualitative methods of inquiry. **Also Known As:** Speech Studies.

Specializations in the Major: Business communications; mass media; sales communication; speech/rhetoric.

Courses Studied in College: English composition; communication theory; introduction to mass media; interpersonal communication; rhetorical tradition and techniques; writing and editing for the media; organizational communication; communication research. **Usual High School Prerequisites:** English; public speaking; foreign language; applied communications; social science.

Related Occupations: Editors (p. 185); Public Relations and Fundraising Managers (p. 246); Public Relations Specialists (p. 247); Radio and Television Announcers (p. 247); Reporters and Correspondents (p. 250); Writers and Authors (p. 266).

Career Paths: This major teaches how effective communication depends on a combination of verbal and nonverbal elements. Students work in various media and learn how to strike a balance between covering the subject matter, appealing to the listener or reader, and projecting the intended image of the speaker or writer. Graduates of communication and speech programs, perhaps with additional education, may go on to careers in sales, public relations, law, or teaching.

COMPARATIVE LITERATURE

see English, p. 111.

COMPUTER ENGINEERING

see Engineering Majors, p. 104.

COMPUTER SCIENCE

Focuses on computer theory, computing problems and solutions, and the design of computer systems and user interfaces from a scientific perspective. Includes instruction in the principles of computational science, computer development and programming, and applications to a variety of end-use situations.

Specializations in the Major: Artificial intelligence; business applications; databases; graphics; human-computer interaction; Internet and mobile applications; security and disaster recovery; systems; robotics.

Courses Studied in College: English composition; calculus; linear algebra; statistics; introduction to computer science; programming in a language (e.g., C, PASCAL, COBOL); algorithms and data structures; software engineering; operating systems; data structures; theory of computation; computer architecture. **Usual High School Prerequisites:** English; algebra; geometry; trigonometry; pre-calculus; calculus; chemistry; physics; computer science.

Related Occupations: Computer and Information Research Scientists (p. 170); Computer and Information Systems Managers (p. 170); Computer Network Support Specialists (p. 173); Computer Occupations,

All Other (p. 173); Computer Programmers (p. 177); Information Security Analysts (p. 208); Software Developers, Applications (p. 254); Software Developers, Systems Software (p. 255); Web Developers (p. 266).

Career Paths: Computer literacy teaches you how to use existing technologies; computer science teaches you how to develop new ones. Several of the fastest-growing occupations are open to those with a bachelor's degree in computer science. Job prospects are excellent for those who can do creative and collaborative work that is not easily outsourced to overseas workers. Systems administration and information security are hot specializations.

CRIMINAL JUSTICE

Prepares individuals to perform the duties of police and public security officers, including patrol and investigative activities, traffic control, crowd control, and public relations, witness interviewing, evidence collection and management, basic crime prevention methods, weapon and equipment operation and maintenance, report preparation, and other routine law enforcement responsibilities. **Also Known As:** Police Science.

Specializations in the Major: Business security; courts/judiciary; corrections; forensic science; homeland security; investigation; law enforcement; police administration; police work.

Courses Studied in College: Introduction to psychology; introduction to criminal justice; introduction to sociology; introduction to criminology; statistics for business and social sciences; criminal procedures; criminal law; juvenile delinquency; police-community relations; ethics, diversity and conflict; seminar (reporting on research). **Usual High School Prerequisites:** Algebra; English; foreign language; social science; history; public speaking; computer science.

Related Occupations: Correctional Officers and Jailers (p. 179); First-Line Supervisors of Correctional Officers (p. 196); First-Line Supervisors of Police and Detectives (p. 198).

Career Paths: This major teaches about the criminal justice system and its agencies, personnel, and historical foundation. Students learn about crime, crime prevention, and public and corporate responses to criminal behaviors on the local, national, and international level. Graduates may find work in business intelligence, corporate security, or homeland security. Those seeking to work as police officers usually earn higher pay than those without this background. Admission to a police academy usually requires meeting physical and psychological requirements.

DANCE

Prepares individuals to express ideas, feelings, and inner visions through the performance of one or more of the dance disciplines, including but not limited to ballet, modern, jazz, ethnic, and folk dance. Focuses on the study and analysis of dance as a cultural phenomenon. Includes instruction in technique, choreography, Laban notation, dance history and criticism, and dance production.

Specializations in the Major: Ballet; ballroom dance; choreography; composite dance; dance education; folk dance; modern dance; tap.

Courses Studied in College: Anatomy and kinesiology for dance; history of dance; dance composition; dance notation; dance technique (e.g., ballet, tap, modern); seminar (reporting on research). **Usual High School Prerequisites:** Biology; foreign language; dance; music.

Related Occupations: Choreographers (p. 164); Dancers (p. 182).

Career Paths: Dancers and choreographers express ideas and stories in performance, using dance. Dancers spend years learning dances and perfecting their skills, usually starting their training at a very early age. When their bodies can no longer take the stresses of performing, they may work instead in dance instruction and choreography. This is a very competitive field. Dancers who attend schools or conservatories associated with a dance company may have a better chance of finding work at that company than others. Job opportunities are better for dance teachers.

DRAMA

see Theater Arts, p. 141.

EARLY CHILDHOOD EDUCATION

see Education Majors, p. 90.

EARTH SCIENCE

see Geology, p. 113.

ECOLOGY

see Environmental Science, p. 111.

ECONOMICS

Focuses on the systematic study of the production, conservation, and allocation of resources in conditions of scarcity, together with the organizational frameworks related to these processes. Includes instruction in economic theory, micro- and macroeconomics, comparative economic systems, money and banking systems, international economics, quantitative analytical methods, and applications to specific industries and public policy issues.

Specializations in the Major: Agricultural; applied; econometrics; environmental; financial; international; political; real estate; theory.

Courses Studied in College: English composition; calculus; introduction to economics; statistics for business and social sciences; introduction to computer science; microeconomic theory; macroeconomic theory; mathematical methods in economics; econometrics; seminar (reporting on research). **Usual High School Prerequisites:** Algebra; English; foreign language; social science; trigonometry; pre-calculus.

Related Occupations: Economists (p. 184); Managers, All Other (p. 215); Survey Researchers (p. 261).

Career Paths: Economics is most basically the study of human needs and how they are satisfied. Economists study the production and distribution of resources, goods, and services by collecting and analyzing data, researching trends, and evaluating economic issues. Many bachelor's degree holders find jobs outside the economist occupation, working instead as research assistants, financial analysts, market analysts, and in similar positions in business, finance, and consulting. Working as an economist usually requires a master's degree or PhD. The best job opportunities should be for those with graduate degrees, working in consulting firms.

EDUCATION MAJORS

EDUCATION (CORE)

For upper-division courses, see the following education specializations.

Lower-Division College Courses: Introduction to psychology; English composition; oral communication; history and philosophy of education; human growth and development; teaching methods; educational psychology; educational alternatives for exceptional students; technology for educators; student teaching.

BUSINESS EDUCATION (UPPER DIVISION)

Prepares individuals to teach vocational business programs at various educational levels.

Specializations in the Major: Distributive education; office skills; technology support.

For lower-division courses, see Education (Core), p. 89.

Upper-Division College Courses: Introduction to accounting; legal environment of business; business finance; introduction to business management; business information processing; statistics for business and social sciences; business reports and communication; introduction to marketing; methods of teaching business subjects. **Usual High School Prerequisites:** English; algebra; geometry; trigonometry; science; foreign language; keyboarding; office computer applications; public speaking.

Related Occupations: Career/Technical Education Teachers, Middle School (p. 159); Career/Technical Education Teachers, Secondary School (p. 160).

Career Paths: Business educators need to know about, and perhaps have work experience in, one or more specific business fields—such as bookkeeping, retailing, or office computer applications—that they will teach. They also need to understand techniques for instruction and for managing the classroom. All states require public high school teachers to have at least a bachelor's degree. Some states require high school teachers to earn a master's degree after earning their teaching certification. Teachers in private schools do not need to meet state requirements, but these schools typically seek teachers who have a bachelor's degree in secondary education. Many jobs will open as baby boomers retire from teaching. Job opportunities may be better in some parts of the country—with higher enrollment rates—such as in the South, West, and rural areas.

EARLY CHILDHOOD EDUCATION (UPPER DIVISION)

Prepares individuals to teach students ranging in age from infancy through eight years (grade 3), depending on the school system or state regulations. Includes preparation to teach all relevant subject matter.

Specializations in the Major: Art education; bilingual education; music education; reading readiness.

For lower-division courses, see Education (Core), p. 89.

Upper-Division College Courses: Emergent literacy; reading assessment and teaching; mathematics education for children; arts education for children; health and physical education for children; science education for children; children's literature. **Usual High School Prerequisites:** English; algebra; geometry; trigonometry; science; foreign language; public speaking.

Related Occupations: Kindergarten Teachers, Except Special Education (p. 212); Preschool Teachers, Except Special Education (p. 241).

Career Paths: In child-care centers, preschool teachers generally are required to have a least a high school diploma and a certification in early childhood education. However, employers may prefer to hire workers with at least some postsecondary education in early childhood education. Preschool teachers in Head Start programs are required to have at least an associate's degree, but the bachelor's degree is becoming a common requirement. Public pre-school teachers in most states and public kindergarten teachers in all states need to have at least a bachelor's degree in early childhood education or elementary education. Many jobs in kindergartens will open as baby boomers retire from teaching, but competition will be keen in some areas of the country. Job prospects should be best in Sunbelt communities. For preschool teachers, a bachelor's degree or certification as a Child Development Associate (CDA) or Child Care Professional (CCP) should be a competitive advantage.

ELEMENTARY EDUCATION (UPPER DIVISION)

Prepares individuals to teach students in the elementary grades, which may include kindergarten through grade 8, depending on the school system or state regulations. Includes preparation to teach all elementary education subject matter.

Specializations in the Major: Art education; bilingual education; mathematics education; music education; reading; science education.

For lower-division courses, see Education (Core), p. 89.

Upper-Division College Courses: Reading assessment and teaching; mathematics education for children; social studies education for children; science education for children; language arts for children; children's literature; classroom management. **Usual High School Prerequisites:** English; algebra; geometry; trigonometry; science; foreign language; public speaking.

Related Occupations: Elementary School Teachers, Except Special Education (p. 187); Middle School Teachers, Except Special and Career/ Technical Education (p. 225).

Career Paths: All states require public elementary school teachers to have at least a bachelor's degree in elementary education. Some states require them to have majored in a content area, such as math or science, with additional classes in education. Some states require all teachers to earn a master's degree after receiving their teaching certification. Teachers in private schools do not need to meet state requirements, but these schools typically seek elementary school teachers who have a bachelor's degree in elementary education. Many jobs will open as baby boomers retire from teaching. On the other hand, competition for openings will be keen in areas of the country that already have a surplus of teachers who are trained to teach elementary school. Job prospects should be best in Sunbelt communities and for those who specialize in teaching English as a second language (ESL) and special education.

FAMILY AND CONSUMER SCIENCES EDUCATION (UPPER DIVISION)

Prepares individuals to teach vocational home economics programs at various educational levels. **Also Known As:** Home Economics Education.

Specializations in the Major: Child care and family life; clothing and textiles; consumer economics and financial planning; consumer merchandising; consumer services and advocacy; foods and nutrition; interior design.

For lower-division courses, see Education (Core), p. 89.

Upper-Division College Courses: Foods; introduction to nutrition; introduction to interior design; marriage and family relationships; family finances; housing; clothing and fashion; parent education. **Usual High School Prerequisites:** English; algebra; geometry; trigonometry; science; foreign language; home economics; public speaking.

Related Occupations: Career/Technical Education Teachers, Middle School (p. 159); Career/Technical Education Teachers, Secondary School (p. 160); Middle School Teachers, Except Special and Career/Technical Education (p. 225); Secondary School Teachers, Except Special and Career/Technical Education (p. 251).

Career Paths: Formerly called home economics education, this major covers a diverse set of specializations and therefore prepares for many different careers besides the main one, education. Some graduates work in industries that market to families, perhaps in sales or marketing research. Some provide financial advice to families. A master's or doctoral degree is needed to teach in college or work for the federal government as a cooperative extension agent.

GIFTED EDUCATION

see Special Education (Upper Division), p. 95.

HOME ECONOMICS EDUCATION

see Family and Consumer Sciences Education (Upper Division), p. 92.

PHYSICAL EDUCATION (UPPER DIVISION)

Prepares individuals to teach physical education programs and to coach sports at various educational levels.

Specializations in the Major: Adapted; aquatics; athletic training; coaching; exercise science; health education; recreation; sports activities.

For lower-division courses, see Education (Core), p. 89.

Upper-Division College Courses: Human anatomy and physiology; history and philosophy of physical education; methods of teaching physical education; kinesiology; adapted physical education; motor learning and development; organization and administration of physical education; assessment in physical education; methods of teaching dance; methods of teaching sports activities; methods of teaching lifetime leisure activities; methods of teaching swimming; personal and community health. **Usual High School Prerequisites:** English; algebra; geometry; trigonometry; science; foreign language; public speaking.

Related Occupations: Coaches and Scouts (p. 168); Fitness Trainers and Aerobics Instructors (p. 199); Middle School Teachers, Except Special and Career/Technical Education (p. 225); Secondary School Teachers, Except Special and Career/Technical Education (p. 251).

Career Paths: Nationwide interest in fitness and health is improving the outlook for physical education graduates, whether as teachers or as instructors and athletic directors in health and sports clubs. Most states require public school teachers to have a bachelor's degree, and some states require them to earn a master's degree after earning their teaching certification. Teachers in private schools do not need to meet state requirements, but these schools typically seek teachers who have a bachelor's degree in education. Many jobs will open as baby boomers retire from teaching, but opportunities will vary by region. Job prospects should be best in Sunbelt communities. An additional master's degree can open an opportunity for a career in athletic training or exercise physiology.

SECONDARY EDUCATION (UPPER DIVISION)

Prepares individuals to teach students in the secondary grades, which may include grades 7 through 12, depending on the school system or state regulations. May include preparation to teach a comprehensive curriculum or specific subject matter.

Specializations in the Major: Art education; bilingual education; language education; mathematics education; music education; remedial and developmental reading; science education; social studies education.

For lower-division courses, see Education (Core), p. 89.

Upper-Division College Courses: Courses in subject to be taught; literacy and assessment in subject to be taught; classroom management. **Usual High School Prerequisites:** English; algebra; geometry; trigonometry; science; forcign language; public speaking.

Related Occupations: Secondary School Teachers, Except Special and Career/Technical Education (p. 251).

Career Paths: All states require public high school teachers to have at least a bachelor's degree. Most states require high school teachers to have majored in a subject area, such as chemistry or history, with additional classes in education. Some states require high school teachers to earn a master's degree after earning their teaching certification. Teachers in private schools do not need to meet state requirements, but these schools typically seek teachers who have a bachelor's degree in secondary education. Many jobs will open as baby boomers retire from teaching. Job prospects should be best in Sunbelt communities and for those who specialize in teaching math, science (especially chemistry and physics), English as a second language, and special education.

SPECIAL EDUCATION
(UPPER DIVISION)

Focuses on the design and provision of teaching and other educational services to children or adults with special learning needs or disabilities and that may prepare individuals to function as special education teachers. Includes instruction in diagnosing learning disabilities, developing individual education plans, teaching and supervising special education students, special education counseling, and applicable laws and policies. **Also Known As:** Gifted Education.

Specializations in the Major: Autism; communication disorders; early childhood; multiple disabilities; orientation and mobility; specific learning disabilities; traumatic brain injury; visual impairments.

For lower-division courses, see Education (Core), p. 89.

Upper-Division College Courses: Curriculum and methods for special education; assessment in special education; classroom management; behavior management; education for moderate and severe disabilities; language development and communication; reading assessment and teaching; mathematics education for children; cultural diversity and disability. **Usual High School Prerequisites:** English; algebra; geometry; trigonometry; science; foreign language; public speaking.

Related Occupations: Special Education Teachers, All Other (p. 256); Special Education Teachers, Kindergarten and Elementary School (p. 257); Special Education Teachers, Middle School (p. 257); Special Education Teachers, Preschool (p. 258); Special Education Teachers, Secondary School (p. 258).

Career Paths: Special education teachers work with students who have a wide range of learning, mental, emotional, and physical disabilities. They adapt general education lessons and teach various subjects to students with mild and moderate disabilities. They also teach basic skills to students with severe disabilities. Some work with gifted students. A bachelor's degree is the minimum requirement, and some who enter this field major in a subject area and minor in special education. In some states, a master's degree is needed for licensure. Job opportunity in this field is expected to be good, especially in high-growth regions and for those who specialize in teaching students with disabilities that are multiple, severe, or on the autism spectrum.

TECHNOLOGY EDUCATION (UPPER DIVISION)

Prepares individuals to teach specific vocational technical education programs at various educational levels.

Specializations in the Major: A technology (such as computers or welding); agriculture.

For lower-division courses, see Education (Core), p. 89.

Upper-Division College Courses: Pre-calculus; evaluation in technical education; instructional materials in technical education; classroom management; special needs in technical education; shop safety; production technology; computer-aided design. **Usual High School Prerequisites:** English; algebra; geometry; trigonometry; science; foreign language; industrial arts; mechanical drawing; public speaking.

Related Occupations: Career/Technical Education Teachers, Middle School (p. 159); Career/Technical Education Teachers, Secondary School (p. 160).

Career Paths: Technology education teachers instruct students in various technical and vocational subjects, such as auto repair, health care, computer science, and culinary arts. As in other teaching fields, a job in a public school usually requires a bachelor's degree, and a master's may be necessary to progress beyond the entry level. Work experience in the technology being taught is valuable, and some public school teachers enter the career based on this experience and on a commitment to work toward a bachelor's. Some technical educators work in postsecondary technical, trade, or business schools. Job opportunities will depend partly on government spending, including financial aid for postsecondary students. Prospects will be better in some specializations, such as health care, than in others.

ELECTRICAL ENGINEERING

see Engineering Majors, p. 105.

ELECTRONICS ENGINEERING

see Engineering Majors, p. 105.

ELEMENTARY EDUCATION

see Education Majors, p. 91.

ENGINEERING MAJORS

ENGINEERING (CORE)

For upper-division courses, see the following engineering specializations.

Lower-Division College Courses: English composition; technical writing; calculus; differential equations; introduction to computer science; general chemistry; general physics; statics; dynamics; engineering graphics; introduction to engineering; numerical analysis. In the upper division, most programs require a senior design project.

AERONAUTICAL/AEROSPACE ENGINEERING (UPPER DIVISION)

Prepares individuals to apply mathematical and scientific principles to the design, development and operational evaluation of aircraft, missiles, space vehicles, and their systems; applied research on flight and orbital characteristics; and the development of systems and procedures for the launching, guidance, and control of air and space vehicles.

Specializations in the Major: Airframes and aerodynamics; avionics; controls; propulsion; spacecraft; structural analysis; systems; testing.

For lower-division courses, see Engineering (Core), p. 98.

Upper-Division College Courses: Thermodynamics; introduction to electric circuits; introduction to aerospace engineering; materials engineering; gas dynamics; aircraft systems and propulsion; flight control systems; aerodynamics; aircraft structural design; experimental aerodynamics; aerospace propulsion; space flight mechanics. **Usual High School Prerequisites:** English; algebra; geometry; trigonometry; pre-calculus; calculus; chemistry; physics; computer science.

Related Occupations: Aerospace Engineers (p. 150); Architectural and Engineering Managers (p. 153).

Career Paths: The career track for aerospace engineers is a bachelor's degree in aerospace engineering or some other field of engineering or science related to aerospace systems. Security clearance is needed to work on projects related to national defense, and that may require U.S. citizenship. A graduate degree will allow an engineer to work as an instructor at a university or to do research and development. Aerospace engineers who know how to use collaborative engineering tools and processes and are familiar with modeling, simulation, and robotics should have good job opportunities. Employment opportunities also should be favorable for those trained in computational fluid dynamics software, which has enabled companies to test designs in a digital environment.

AGRICULTURAL ENGINEERING (UPPER DIVISION)

Prepares individuals to apply mathematical and scientific principles to the design, development and operational evaluation of systems, equipment and facilities for production, processing, storage, handling, distribution and use of food, feed, and fiber. Includes applications to aquaculture, forestry, human and natural resources.

Specializations in the Major: Environmental engineering; food and fiber processing; irrigation and drainage; mechanization; soil conservation; structures.

For lower-division courses, see Engineering (Core), p. 98.

Upper-Division College Courses: General biology; introduction to electric circuits; thermodynamics; introduction to agricultural engineering; engineering properties of biological materials; fluid mechanics; soil and water engineering; agricultural power and machines; biological materials processing. **Usual High School Prerequisites:** English; algebra; geometry; trigonometry; pre-calculus; biology; calculus; chemistry; computer science.

Related Occupations: Agricultural Engineers (p. 151); Architectural and Engineering Managers (p. 153).

Career Paths: Agricultural engineers work on activities ranging from aquaculture to land farming or forestry; from developing biofuels to improving conservation; and from planning animal environments to finding better ways to process food. They must have a bachelor's degree, preferably in agricultural engineering or biological engineering. Employers also value practical experience, so cooperative-education engineering programs at universities are valuable as well. Best job opportunities may be in new areas related to agriculture, such as high-tech applications for agricultural products, water resource management, alternative energies, and design of new machinery and equipment for agriculture.

BIOENGINEERING
(UPPER DIVISION)

Prepares individuals to apply mathematical and scientific principles to the design, development and operational evaluation of biomedical and health systems and products such as integrated biomedical systems, instrumentation, medical information systems, artificial organs and prostheses, and health management and care delivery systems. **Also Known As:** Biomedical Engineering.

Specializations in the Major: Bioinstrumentation; biomaterials; biomechanics; biomedical engineering; clinical engineering; computational bioengineering; genomics; medical imaging;

nanotechnology; prosthetics and artificial organs; rehabilitation engineering; robotic surgery.

For lower-division courses, see Engineering (Core), p. 98.

Upper-Division College Courses: Introduction to electric circuits; general biology; organic chemistry; cell biology; introduction to bioengineering; thermodynamics; bioinstrumentation; biomaterials; biomechanics. **Usual High School Prerequisites:** English; algebra; geometry; trigonometry; pre-calculus; calculus; chemistry; biology; physics; computer science.

Related Occupations: Architectural and Engineering Managers (p. 153); Biomedical Engineers (p. 158).

Career Paths: Biomedical engineers work in manufacturing, universities, hospitals, research facilities of companies and educational and medical institutions, and government regulatory agencies. Some get a bachelor's degree in a different field of engineering and then either get a graduate degree in biomedical engineering or get on-the-job training in biomedical engineering. To lead a research team, a biomedical engineer typically needs a graduate degree. Some biomedical engineers attend dental or medical school to specialize in applications at the forefront of patient care, such as using electric impulses in new ways to get muscles moving again. Some earn law degrees and work as patent attorneys. Rapid advances in technology will continue to change what biomedical engineers do and will continue to create new areas for them to work in. Thus, the expanding range of work activities should translate into very favorable job prospects. In addition, the aging and retirement of a substantial percentage of biomedical engineers are likely to help create job openings.

BIOMEDICAL ENGINEERING

see Bioengineering (Upper Division), p. 100.

CHEMICAL ENGINEERING (UPPER DIVISION)

Prepares individuals to apply mathematical and scientific principles to the design, development and operational evaluation of systems employing chemical processes, such as chemical reactors, kinetic systems, electrochemical systems, energy conservation processes, heat and mass transfer systems, and separation processes; and the applied analysis of chemical problems such as corrosion, particle abrasion, energy loss, pollution, and fluid mechanics.

Specializations in the Major: Bioengineering; energy economics; mathematical modeling and simulation; microchemical and microfluidic systems; nuclear engineering; pharmaceuticals; pollution; polymers; quality control.

For lower-division courses, see Engineering (Core), p. 98.

Upper-Division College Courses: Organic chemistry; introduction to chemical engineering; thermodynamics; materials engineering; chemical engineering thermodynamics; kinetics and reactor design; process mass transfer; process heat transfer; process dynamics and controls; separations processes; process design and optimization. **Usual High School Prerequisites:** English; algebra; geometry; trigonometry; pre-calculus; calculus; chemistry; physics; computer science.

Related Occupations: Architectural and Engineering Managers (p. 153); Chemical Engineers (p. 160).

Career Paths: Chemical engineers apply the principles of chemistry, biology, physics, and math to solve problems that involve the production or use of chemicals, fuel, drugs, food, and many other products. They must have a bachelor's degree in chemical engineering. Employers also value practical experience, so cooperative engineering programs, in which students earn college credit for structured job experience, are valuable as well. A graduate degree allows an engineer to work in research and development or as a postsecondary teacher. Overall job growth will be tempered by a decline in employment in manufacturing sectors, including chemical manufacturing. Best opportunities may be in new fields, such as nanotechnology, alternative energies, and biotechnology.

CIVIL ENGINEERING (UPPER DIVISION)

Prepares individuals to apply mathematical and scientific principles to the design, development and operational evaluation of structural, load-bearing, material moving, transportation, water resource, and material control systems; and environmental safety measures.

Specializations in the Major: Construction; environment; geotechnics; materials; structures; transportation; water resources.

For lower-division courses, see Engineering (Core), p. 98.

Upper-Division College Courses: Introduction to electric circuits; introduction to civil engineering; fluid mechanics; engineering surveying and measurement; environmental engineering and design; soil mechanics; highway and transportation engineering; water resources and hydraulic engineering; geotechnical engineering; civil engineering materials. **Usual High School Prerequisites:** English; algebra; geometry; trigonometry; pre-calculus; calculus; chemistry; physics; computer science.

Related Occupations: Architectural and Engineering Managers (p. 153); Civil Engineers (p. 164); Construction Managers (p. 178).

Career Paths: Civil engineers need a bachelor's degree to enter the field and typically need a graduate degree and licensure for promotion to senior positions. Though licensure requirements vary within the U.S., civil engineers must usually be licensed in the locations where they provide services publicly. Job applicants who gain experience by participating in a co-op program while in college will have the best opportunities. Although states continue to face financial challenges and may have difficulty funding all the infrastructure projects that need attention, some of the projects that have been delayed will ultimately have to be completed.

COMPUTER ENGINEERING
(UPPER DIVISION)

Prepares individuals to apply mathematical and scientific principles to the design, development and operational evaluation of computer hardware and software systems and related equipment and facilities; and the analysis of specific problems of computer applications to various tasks.

Specializations in the Major: Architecture and design; bioengineering; digital signal processing; electromagnetics and photonics; embedded systems; mechatronics; multimedia; networking; systems analysis.

For lower-division courses, see Engineering (Core), p. 98.

Upper-Division College Courses: Introduction to electric circuits; engineering circuit analysis; introduction to signal processing; electronics; microelectronic circuits; computer architecture; algorithms and data structures; digital system design; operating systems. **Usual High School Prerequisites:** English; algebra; geometry; trigonometry; pre-calculus; calculus; chemistry; physics; computer science.

Related Occupations: Architectural and Engineering Managers (p. 153); Computer Hardware Engineers (p. 171); Computer Network Architects (p. 172); Software Developers, Applications (p. 254); Software Developers, Systems Software (p. 255).

Career Paths: Computer hardware engineers research, design, develop, and test computer systems and components such as processors, circuit boards, memory devices, networks, and routers. Some design noncomputer devices that incorporate processors and other computer components and connect to the Internet. Some people who do advanced work with software may have the job title of "engineer," even though their education is in computer science rather than in engineering. Most entry-level computer hardware engineers have a bachelor's degree from an accredited computer engineering program. Some large firms or specialized jobs require a master's degree in computer engineering. All engineers must continue their learning over the course of their careers to keep up with rapid advances in technology. Engineers who have a higher-level degree and knowledge or experience with computer software will have the best job prospects.

ELECTRICAL ENGINEERING (UPPER DIVISION)

Prepares individuals to apply mathematical and scientific principles to the design, development, and operational evaluation of electrical and electronic systems and their components, including electrical power generation systems; and the analysis of problems such as superconductor, wave propagation, energy storage and retrieval, and reception and amplification. **Also Known As:** Electronics Engineering.

Specializations in the Major: Aerospace applications; broadcasting; communications; computer hardware and software; controls; digital signal processing; electromagnetics; optics; power systems; remote sensing; semiconductor devices.

For lower-division courses, see Engineering (Core), p. 98.

Upper-Division College Courses: Engineering circuit analysis; signals and systems; semiconductor devices; digital circuit design; electromagnetic fields; digital communication systems; control systems; electromechanical and electromagnetic energy. **Usual High School Prerequisites:** English; algebra; geometry; trigonometry; pre-calculus; calculus; chemistry; physics; computer science.

Related Occupations: Aerospace Engineers (p. 150); Architectural and Engineering Managers (p. 153); Electrical Engineers (p. 186); Electronics Engineers, Except Computer (p. 186).

Career Paths: Both electrical and electronics engineers must have a bachelor's degree. Employers also value practical experience, so participation in cooperative engineering programs, in which students earn academic credit for structured work experience, is valuable as well. Having a Professional Engineer (PE) license may improve an engineer's chances of finding employment. The rapid pace of technological innovation and development will likely drive demand for electrical and electronics engineers in research and development, as opposed to manufacturing. Computer systems design continues to be a hot field, where workers are needed to implement more powerful portable computing devices.

ELECTRONICS ENGINEERING

see Electrical Engineering (Upper Division), p. 105.

INDUSTRIAL ENGINEERING (UPPER DIVISION)

Prepares individuals to apply scientific and mathematical principles to the design, improvement, and installation of integrated systems of people, material, information, and energy. Includes instruction in applied mathematics, physical sciences, the social sciences, engineering analysis, systems design, computer applications, and forecasting and evaluation methodology. **Also Known As:** Operations Research.

Specializations in the Major: Decision science/operations research; health systems; human factors and ergonomics; manufacturing and production systems; quality management; valuation.

For lower-division courses, see Engineering (Core), p. 98.

Upper-Division College Courses: Engineering statistics; thermodynamics; engineering economics; human factors and ergonomics; engineering systems design; operations research; quality control; facilities design; simulation; analysis of industrial activities; manufacturing processes. **Usual High School Prerequisites:** English; algebra; geometry; trigonometry; pre-calculus; calculus; chemistry; physics; computer science.

Related Occupations: Architectural and Engineering Managers (p. 153); Industrial Engineers (p. 204); Industrial Production Managers (p. 205).

Career Paths: Industrial engineers devise efficient ways to use workers, machines, materials, information, and energy to make a product or provide a service. Some of them focus on safety or quality control. Employers expect a bachelor's degree, typically in industrial engineering. However, many industrial engineers have degrees in mechanical engineering, manufacturing engineering, industrial engineering technology, or general engineering. Employers value experience, so cooperative education engineering programs at universities are also valuable. A graduate degree allows an engineer to work as a professor at a college or university or to engage in research and development. Although projected job growth is slower than the average for all occupations, the versatility of these engineers allows them to target high-growth industries such as health care. Firms in a variety of industries are seeking new ways to contain costs and improve efficiency to compete in the global marketplace.

MATERIALS ENGINEERING

see Metallurgical Engineering (Upper Division), p. 108.

MECHANICAL ENGINEERING (UPPER DIVISION)

Prepares individuals to apply mathematical and scientific principles to the design, development, and operational evaluation of physical systems used in manufacturing and end-product systems used for specific uses, including machine tools, jigs, and other manufacturing equipment; stationary power units and appliances; engines; self-propelled vehicles; housings and containers; hydraulic and electric systems for controlling movement; and the integration of computers and remote control with operating systems.

Specializations in the Major: Automotive design; bioengineering; energy and the environment; heating and air conditioning; manufacturing; mechatronics; nanotechnology; naval architecture; product development; robotics.

For lower-division courses, see Engineering (Core), p. 98.

Upper-Division College Courses: Thermodynamics; fluid mechanics; materials science; materials engineering; mechanical engineering design; computer-aided drafting (CAD); heat transfer; manufacturing processes; dynamic systems. **Usual High School Prerequisites:** English; algebra; geometry; trigonometry; pre-calculus; calculus; chemistry; physics; computer science.

Related Occupations: Aerospace Engineers (p. 150); Architectural and Engineering Managers (p. 153); Cost Estimators (p. 179); Mechanical Engineers (p. 222).

Career Paths: Mechanical engineering is one of the broadest engineering disciplines. Mechanical engineers design, develop, build, and test mechanical and thermal devices, including tools, engines, and machines. Employers expect a bachelor's degree, and a graduate degree is typically needed to conduct research. Mechanical engineers who sell services publicly must be licensed in all states and the District of Columbia. Most employers prefer to hire students from an accredited program, and programs that include internships and co-ops may require extra years but can better prepare students for work in industry. Some of the industries where mechanical engineers can find the best job opportunities are architectural, engineering, and related service firms; some manufacturing industries, such as transportation equipment and machinery manufacturing (especially robotic machines); and oil and gas extraction. Prospects will be best for grads with training in the latest software tools and 3D printing.

METALLURGICAL ENGINEERING (UPPER DIVISION)

Prepares individuals to apply mathematical and metallurgical principles to the design, development, and operational evaluation of metal components of structural, load-bearing, power, transmission, and moving systems; and the analysis of engineering problems such as stress, creep, failure, alloy behavior, environmental fluctuations, stability, electromagnetic and thermodynamic characteristics, optimal manufacturing processes, and related design considerations. **Also Known As:** Materials Engineering.

Specializations in the Major: Chemical metallurgy; extraction; materials research; physical metallurgy; process engineering.

For lower-division courses, see Engineering (Core), p. 98.

Upper-Division College Courses: Thermodynamics; materials engineering; materials thermodynamics; metallurgical transport; metallurgical design; engineering statistics; manufacturing processes; physical metallurgy. **Usual High School Prerequisites:** English; algebra; geometry; trigonometry; pre-calculus; calculus; chemistry; physics; computer science.

Related Occupations: Architectural and Engineering Managers (p. 153); Materials Engineers (p. 220).

Career Paths: Metallurgical engineers develop, process, and test metallic materials to meet certain mechanical, electrical, and chemical requirements. They may work in teams with scientists and engineers from other backgrounds. They typically have a bachelor's degree in metallurgical engineering, materials science, or a related field. Employers also value practical experience. Therefore, cooperative engineering programs, which provide college credit for structured job experience, are valuable as well. Some colleges and universities offer a five-year program leading to both a bachelor's and master's degree. A graduate degree allows an engineer to work as an instructor at some colleges and universities or to do research and development. Some employers prefer to hire candidates who have graduated from an accredited program. Despite a projected slow growth rate for materials engineers, job prospects should be favorable, especially for those educated in metallurgical engineering.

OPERATIONS RESEARCH

see Industrial Engineering (Upper Division), p. 106.

PETROLEUM ENGINEERING (UPPER DIVISION)

Prepares individuals to apply mathematical and scientific principles to the design, development, and operational evaluation of systems for locating, extracting, processing and refining crude petroleum and natural gas, including prospecting instruments and equipment, mining and drilling systems, processing and refining systems and facilities, storage facilities, transportation systems, and related environmental and safety systems.

Specializations in the Major: Distribution; drilling; exploration; facilities; refining; production; reservoirs; well-log analysis.

For lower-division courses, see Engineering (Core), p. 98.

Upper-Division College Courses: Physical geology; sedimentary rocks and processes; petroleum geology; fluid mechanics; thermodynamics; heat transfer; materials engineering; engineering economics; formation evaluation; drilling engineering; petroleum production engineering; natural gas engineering; reservoir engineering; well testing and analysis; well stimulation; secondary recovery. **Usual High School Prerequisites:** English; algebra; geometry; trigonometry; pre-calculus; calculus; chemistry; physics; computer science.

Related Occupations: Architectural and Engineering Managers (p. 153); Petroleum Engineers (p. 233).

Career Paths: Petroleum engineers must have a bachelor's degree in engineering, preferably in petroleum engineering. However, a bachelor's degree in mechanical or chemical engineering may also suffice. Employers also value work experience, so cooperative education programs, in which students earn academic credit for structured job experience, are valuable as well. Some colleges and universities offer a five-year program in chemical or mechanical engineering that leads to both a bachelor's degree and a master's degree. Some employers may prefer applicants who have earned a graduate degree. A graduate degree also allows an engineer to work as an instructor at some universities or in research and development. Job prospects are expected to be highly favorable.

ENGLISH

Focuses on the English language, including its history, structure and related communications skills; and the literature and culture of English-speaking peoples. **Also Known As:** Literature.

Specializations in the Major: A literary genre; a literary period; creative writing; English education; language; literary criticism; rhetoric.

Courses Studied in College: English composition; introduction to literary study; foreign language; survey of British literature; survey of American literature; a genre (e.g., drama, short story, poetry); comparative literature; seminar (reporting on research). **Usual High School Prerequisites:** English; foreign language; literature; history; public speaking; social science.

Related Occupations: Editors (p. 185); Public Relations and Fundraising Managers (p. 246); Public Relations Specialists (p. 247); Secondary School Teachers, Except Special and Career/Technical Education (p. 251); Writers and Authors (p. 266).

Career Paths: English majors develop first-rate writing and critical-thinking skills that can be valuable in a variety of careers. Journalism, public relations, advertising, and law (with an appropriate postgraduate degree) are fields where these skills are prized. They also are known to make excellent trainees in computer programming. Some get a master's in teaching. Because the degree is not as career-oriented as many others, graduates usually have to make a greater effort to convince employers that they are good job candidates. They can improve their chances by harnessing their research and writing skills for active and creative job-hunting.

ENVIRONMENTAL SCIENCE

Focuses on the application of biological, chemical, and physical principles to the study of the physical environment and the solution of environmental problems, including subjects such as abating or controlling environmental pollution and degradation; the interaction between human society and the natural environment; and natural resources management. Includes instruction in biology, chemistry, physics, geosciences, climatology, statistics, and mathematical modeling. **Also Known As:** Ecology.

Specializations in the Major: Aquatic biology; Earth systems; environmental education; environmental policy; environmental technology; land resources; ; natural history soil ecology.

Courses Studied in College: English composition; calculus; general biology; general chemistry; organic chemistry; statistics; introduction to computer science; introduction to geology; introduction to soil science; ecology and evolution; introduction to environmental science; environmental management; introduction to economics; introduction to ground water/hydrology; environmental impact assessment; environmental chemistry; land use and environmental policy. **Usual High School Prerequisites:** Biology; chemistry; algebra; geometry; trigonometry; computer science; English; public speaking; geography.

Related Occupations: Environmental Scientists and Specialists, Including Health (p. 188).

Career Paths: Industries are feeling pressure to take responsibility for maintaining a sustainable environment. To that end, they are creating positions dealing with waste management, pollution reduction, and other environmental responsibilities. Graduates who hold a bachelor's degree in this field may get an entry-level job with an environmental consulting business or a government planning agency. A master's degree may be needed for advancement. The relatively few jobs in college teaching and basic research usually require a doctoral degree, but opportunities are probably better for those whose advanced degree is in a particular scientific field, such as chemistry or geology, rather than in this interdisciplinary field.

FAMILY AND CONSUMER SCIENCES EDUCATION

see Education Majors, p. 92.

FINANCE

see Business Majors, p. 75.

FINE ART

see Studio Art, p. 140.

FRENCH

see Modern Foreign Language, p. 124.

GENDER STUDIES

see Area Studies, p. 68.

GENETICS

see Biology, p. 71.

GEOLOGY

Focuses on the scientific study of the earth; the forces acting upon it; and the behavior of the solids, liquids and gases comprising it. Includes instruction in historical geology, geomorphology, and sedimentology, the chemistry of rocks and soils, stratigraphy, mineralogy, petrology, geostatistics, volcanology, glaciology, geophysical principles, and applications to research and industrial problems. **Also Known As:** Earth Science; Planetary Science.

Specializations in the Major: Engineering geology; environment; exploration; geochemistry; geographic information systems; geophysics; hydrogeology; mineralogy; oceanography; paleontology; petroleum geology; remote sensing; stratigraphy; tectonics; volcanology.

Courses Studied in College: English composition; calculus; introduction to computer science; general chemistry; general physics; introduction to geology; invertebrate paleontology; vertebrate paleontology; field geology; structural geology; physical geology; mineralogy; igneous and metamorphic petrology; sedimentation and stratigraphy. **Usual High School Prerequisites:** English; algebra; geometry; trigonometry; chemistry; physics; pre-calculus; computer science; calculus.

Related Occupations: Geoscientists, Except Hydrologists and Geographers (p. 201); Hydrologists (p. 204); Natural Sciences Managers (p. 227).

Career Paths: Geology is the study of the physical aspects of Earth, such as its composition, structure, and processes, to learn about its past, present, and future. Geologists use knowledge of this field to locate resources; to protect the environment; and to offer advice on construction and land-use projects. Most geologist jobs require at least a bachelor's degree. In several states, geoscientists need a license to offer their services to the public. Job opportunities should be excellent for geologists, particularly those who earn a master's degree. Most opportunities are expected to be related to resource extraction—in particular, gas and oil exploration and extraction operations.

GERMAN

see Modern Foreign Language, p. 124.

GIFTED EDUCATION

see Education Majors, p. 95.

GOVERNMENT

see Political Science, p. 129.

GRAPHIC DESIGN

Prepares individuals to apply artistic and computer techniques to the interpretation of technical and commercial concepts. Includes instruction in computer-assisted art and design, printmaking, concepts sketching, technical drawing, color theory, imaging, studio technique, still and life modeling, multimedia applications, communication skills and commercial art business operations. **Also Known As:** Illustration.

Specializations in the Major: Animation and cartooning; digital media; illustration; letterform; print media; typography; webpage design.

Courses Studied in College: English composition; basic drawing; art history: prehistoric to Renaissance; art history: Renaissance to modern; introduction to graphic design; visual concepts; history of graphic design; two-dimensional design; three-dimensional design; typography; computer graphics; senior design project; digital photography; introduction to multimedia. **Usual High School Prerequisites:** Algebra; geometry; trigonometry; pre-calculus; English; public speaking; art; computer science; mechanical drawing; photography.

Related Occupations: Art Directors (p. 155); Artists and Related Workers, All Other (p. 155); Graphic Designers (p. 201); Multimedia Artists and Animators (p. 226).

Career Paths: Graphic designers create visual concepts, by hand or using computer software, to communicate ideas that inspire, inform, or captivate consumers. They develop the overall layout and production design for advertisements, brochures, magazines, and corporate reports. Besides gaining understanding of design concepts, students in this major assemble a portfolio of work to show prospective employers. Many graduates with a bachelor's degree work for publishers and design firms. Some freelance. Job prospects will be better for job applicants who work with various types of media, such as websites and print publications. Experienced graphic designers may advance to chief designer, art or creative director, or other supervisory positions.

HEALTH ADMINISTRATION

see Health Facilities Administration, p. 116.

HEALTH FACILITIES ADMINISTRATION

Prepares individuals to apply managerial principles to the administration of hospitals, clinics, nursing homes, and other health care facilities. Includes instruction in facilities planning, building and operations management, business management, financial management and insurance, fund-raising and marketing, public relations, human resources management and labor relations, health care facilities operations, principles of health-care delivery, and applicable law and regulations. **Also Known As:** Health Administration; Hospital Administration.

Specializations in the Major: Health policy; health-care informatics; hospital management; long-term care management.

Courses Studied in College: English composition; introduction to economics; college algebra; oral communication; accounting; introduction to business management; statistics for business and social sciences; American health-care systems; introduction to medical terminology; epidemiology; introduction to management information systems; financial management of health care; human resource management in health-care facilities; strategy and planning for health care; legal aspects of health care; health care and politics; managed care; research methodologies in health care; field experience/internship. **Usual High School Prerequisites:** Algebra; English; geometry; trigonometry; pre-calculus; biology; chemistry; computer science; office computer applications; public speaking; social science; foreign language.

Related Occupations: Medical and Health Services Managers (p. 224).

Career Paths: Graduates of this program may manage an entire facility or specialize in managing a specific clinical area or department; they also may manage a medical practice for a group of physicians. Some programs in this field allow students to specialize in a particular type of facility. All states require nursing care facility administrators to be licensed; requirements vary by state. Certification also is available in many areas of practice, such as health information management or medical management. Demand for managers of medical group practice management is expected to grow as medical group practices become larger and more complex.

HEBREW

see Modern Foreign Language, p. 124.

HINDI

see Modern Foreign Language, p. 124.

HISTORY

Focuses on the general study and interpretation of the past, including the gathering, recording, synthesizing and criticizing of evidence and theories about past events. Includes instruction in historiography; historical research methods; studies of specific periods, issues and cultures; and applications to areas such as historic preservation, public policy, and records administration.

Specializations in the Major: A period; a region; applied history; genealogy; history education.

Courses Studied in College: English composition; foreign language; world history to the early modern era; world history in the modern era; American history; theory and practice of history; seminar (reporting on research). **Usual High School Prerequisites:** Algebra; English; foreign language; social science; trigonometry; history.

Related Occupations: Archivists (p. 154); Historians (p. 202); Managers, All Other (p. 215); Secondary School Teachers, Except Special and Career/Technical Education (p. 251).

Career Paths: Historians research, analyze, interpret, and present the past by studying a variety of historical documents and sources. Because history majors get broad training and education in writing, analytical research, and critical thinking, graduates can apply their skills to many different occupations—for example, as writers and authors, editors, postsecondary teachers, high school teachers, or policy analysts. Many history-related jobs do not have the title of historian, and these are more open to those without a doctoral degree. Graduates work as archivists, curators, and museum workers, social science or humanities researchers, and cultural resource managers. Some graduates use the critical-thinking skills they develop from history to go into law.

HOME ECONOMICS EDUCATION

see Family and Consumer Sciences Education (Upper Division) in Education Majors, p. 92.

HOSPITAL ADMINISTRATION

see Health Facilities Administration, p. 116.

HOSPITALITY MANAGEMENT

see Business Majors, p. 76.

HOTEL MANAGEMENT

see Business Majors, p. 76.

HUMAN RESOURCES MANAGEMENT

see Business Majors, p. 77.

ILLUSTRATION

see Graphic Design, p. 114.

INDUSTRIAL ENGINEERING

see Engineering Majors, p. 106.

INSURANCE

see Business Majors, p. 81.

ITALIAN

see Modern Foreign Language, p. 124.

JAPANESE

see Modern Foreign Language, p. 124.

JOURNALISM

Focuses on the theory and practice of gathering, processing, and delivering news and that prepares individuals to be professional print journalists, news editors, and news managers. Includes instruction in news writing and editing; reporting; photojournalism; layout and graphic design; journalism law and policy; professional standards and ethics; research methods; and journalism history and criticism.

Specializations in the Major: Design and graphics; digital and interactive media; media management; news editing and editorializing; news reporting; photojournalism; radio and television news; science and environment; sports.

Courses Studied in College: English composition; American government; introduction to economics; foreign language; introduction to mass media; news writing and reporting; copy editing; media law; media ethics; photojournalism; journalism and society; visual design for media; journalism research; multimedia journalism; journalism practicum.
Usual High School Prerequisites: English; algebra; foreign language; art; literature; public speaking; social science.

Related Occupations: Broadcast News Analysts (p. 158); Editors (p. 185); Public Relations and Fundraising Managers (p. 246); Public

Relations Specialists (p. 247); Reporters and Correspondents (p. 250); Writers and Authors (p. 266).

Career Paths: A journalism program can prepare you to work as a reporter, correspondent, or broadcast news analysts, but it also can lead to work in advertising and public relations. Entry-level journalists are expected to face strong competition for jobs, because of both the number of workers who are interested in entering the field and projected employment declines. Those with experience in the field—for example, from internships—should have the best job prospects. Competition for jobs in advertising and public relations is also expected to be intense. Experience with multimedia or in website design and coding should improve job prospects in all of these fields.

LANDSCAPE ARCHITECTURE

Prepares individuals for the independent professional practice of landscape architecture and research in various aspects of the field. Includes instruction in geology and hydrology; soils, groundcovers, and horticultural elements; project and site planning; landscape design, history, and theory; environmental design; applicable law and regulations; and professional responsibilities and standards.

Specializations in the Major: Arid lands; design; eco-tourism; heritage conservation; historical and cultural landscapes; international studies; land development planning; park and recreation planning; reclamation and restoration; site planning; sustainability; urban design.

Courses Studied in College: Technical writing; pre-calculus; basic drawing; introduction to plant science; introduction to soil science; architectural computer graphics; ecology and evolution; history of landscape architecture; landscape architectural design; GIS and digital design tools; design communication; site engineering; introduction to horticulture; plant materials; site construction and materials and methods; land planning; professional practice of landscape architecture. **Usual High School Prerequisites:** English; algebra; geometry; trigonometry; pre-calculus; calculus; physics; computer science; art; biology.

Related Occupations: Architectural and Engineering Managers (p. 153); Landscape Architects (p. 213).

Career Paths: The career track is either a bachelor's degree or a three-year master's degree program in landscape architecture. To become licensed, candidates must meet experience requirements determined by each state. New hires are called apprentices or intern landscape architects until they become licensed. Good job opportunities are expected overall, especially for those who have strong technical and communication skills and an in-depth knowledge of environmental codes and regulations.

LATIN AMERICAN STUDIES

see Area Studies, p. 68.

LGBT STUDIES

see Area Studies, p. 68.

LIFE SCIENCES

see Biology, p. 71.

LITERATURE

see English, p. 111.

MANAGEMENT INFORMATION SYSTEMS

see Business Majors, p. 79.

MARKETING

see Business Majors, p. 80.

MATERIALS ENGINEERING

see Engineering Majors, p. 108.

MATHEMATICS

Focuses on the analysis of quantities, magnitudes, forms, and their relationships, using symbolic logic and language. Includes instruction in algebra, calculus, functional analysis, geometry, number theory, logic, topology and other mathematical specializations.

Specializations in the Major: Applied and computational; mathematical finance; mathematical statistics; mathematics education; modeling; theoretical mathematics.

Courses Studied in College: Calculus; differential equations; introduction to computer science; programming in a language (e.g., C, PASCAL, COBOL); discrete math; linear algebra; introduction to abstract mathematics. **Usual High School Prerequisites:** Algebra; geometry; trigonometry; pre-calculus; calculus; computer science; physics.

Related Occupations: Mathematical Science Occupations, All Other (p. 221); Mathematicians (p. 221); Natural Sciences Managers (p. 227); Secondary School Teachers, Except Special and Career/ Technical Education (p. 251); Statisticians (p. 260).

Career Paths: Many mathematics majors apply their knowledge by getting additional education or training in a math-intense field, either in a master's program or on the job. For example, an insurance company might train them in actuarial science; a computer consulting company might train them in computer security; a bank might train them in financial modeling; or they might get a graduate degree in economics, engineering, or accounting. A master's degree in teaching opens the door to a career in public schools, and some districts are so hard-pressed for math teachers that they hire math graduates, who subsequently take the required courses in education. Employment opportunities are very good for people who apply mathematical knowledge to other fields. Those who pursue a graduate degree in math may find work in college teaching or at the National Security Agency.

MECHANICAL ENGINEERING

see Engineering Majors, p. 107.

MEDICAL TECHNOLOGY

Prepares individuals to conduct and supervise complex medical tests, clinical trials, and research experiments; manage clinical laboratories; and consult with physicians and clinical researchers on diagnoses, disease causation and spread, and research outcomes. Includes instruction in the theory and practice of hematology, clinical chemistry, microbiology, immunology, immunohematology, physiological relationships to test results, laboratory procedures and quality assurance controls, test and research design and implementation, analytic techniques, laboratory management, data development and reporting, medical informatics, and professional standards and regulations. **Also Known As:** Clinical Laboratory Science.

Specializations in the Major: Blood banking; body fluid analysis; clinical chemistry; clinical microbiology; hematology; immunology.

Courses Studied in College: English composition; general biology; general chemistry; organic chemistry; general physics; human anatomy and physiology; general microbiology; introduction to biochemistry; college algebra; introduction to computer science; statistics; body fluid analysis; parasitology; clinical chemistry; hematology; clinical microbiology; immunohematology; clinical immunology; clinical laboratory management. **Usual High School Prerequisites:** Algebra; biology; chemistry; computer science; English; physics; geometry; trigonometry.

Related Occupations: Medical and Clinical Laboratory Technologists (p. 223).

Career Paths: This bachelor's degree program (sometimes called medical laboratory science) is appropriate preparation for a career as a medical laboratory technologist. Some students learn the specific skills in a hospital-based program during their senior year of college or after having received a bachelor's degree in another science, such as chemistry or biology. Technicians usually need an associate's degree or a postsecondary certificate. Some states require technologists and technicians to be licensed, and in some states this requires certification. Certification is not required to enter the occupation in all cases, but employers typically prefer to hire certified technologists and technicians. An increase in the aging population will lead to a greater need to diagnose medical conditions, such as cancer or type 2 diabetes, through laboratory procedures. Medical laboratory technologists will be in demand to use and maintain the equipment needed for diagnosis and treatment. Expanded health insurance will increase the number of patients who have access to medical care. As a result, demand for the services of laboratory personnel will grow.

METALLURGICAL ENGINEERING

see Engineering Majors, p. 108.

MICROBIOLOGY

see Biology, p. 71.

MIS

see Business Majors, p. 79.

MODERN FOREIGN LANGUAGE

Focuses on one or more modern foreign languages.

Also Known As: Arabic; Chinese; French; German; Hebrew; Hindi; Italian; Japanese; Portuguese; Russian; Spanish.

Specializations in the Major: History and culture of language speakers; language education; linguistics; literature; regional studies; translation.

Courses Studied in College: Foreign language; conversation; composition; linguistics; foreign literature and culture; grammar; phonetics; history of a world region; seminar (reporting on research). **Usual High School Prerequisites:** English; public speaking; foreign language; history; social science.

Related Occupations: Interpreters and Translators (p. 211); Secondary School Teachers, Except Special and Career/Technical Education (p. 251).

Career Paths: Today's global economy is creating many job opportunities for graduates of foreign language programs. Additional course work or a graduate degree in a career-related field such as business, engineering, or agriculture can be helpful. One way to choose a language major is to consider the nations where Americans do the most business or tourism. This partly explains the popularity of majors in Chinese, French, German, Japanese, and Spanish. But there may be less competition for jobs involving the languages studied in the less-common majors, such as Arabic, Hebrew, Hindi, Korean, Portuguese, Swahili, or Turkish, to name just a few. Besides jobs in business, government, and nonprofit organizations, work in translation or college teaching is an option for those with a graduate degree. A brief certification program can lead to work in medical or legal interpreting.

MOTEL MANAGEMENT

see Business Majors, p. 76.

NURSING (RN TRAINING)

Prepares individuals in the knowledge, techniques, and procedures for promoting health, providing care for sick, disabled, infirmed, or other individuals or groups. Includes instruction in the administration of medication and treatments, assisting a physician during treatments and examinations, referring patients to physicians and other health-care specialists, and planning education for health maintenance.

Specializations in the Major: Ambulatory care; administration; community health; hospice and palliative care; mental health; obstetric; pediatric.

Courses Studied in College: English composition; introduction to psychology; introduction to sociology; oral communication; general chemistry; general biology; statistics; human anatomy and physiology; human growth and development; clinical microbiology; ethics in health care; patient examination and evaluation; pharmacology; women's health; pediatric nursing; clinical experience in health information; adult health nursing; mental health nursing; nursing leadership and management; community health nursing; clinical nursing experience. **Usual High School Prerequisites:** English; algebra; geometry; trigonometry; biology; computer science; public speaking; chemistry; foreign language.

Related Occupations: Registered Nurses (p. 248).

Career Paths: Registered nurses (RNs) provide and coordinate patient care, educate patients and the public about various health conditions, and provide advice and emotional support to patients and their family members. Registered nurses usually take one of three education paths: a bachelor's of science degree in nursing (BSN), an associate's degree in nursing (ADN), or a diploma from an approved nursing program. RNs also must be licensed. Some RNs get additional training and become advanced practice registered nurses (APRNs): nurse anesthetists, nurse midwives, or nurse practitioners. In addition to what RNs do, they may also provide primary and specialty health care; the scope of practice varies from state to state. APRNs must earn at least a master's degree in one of the specialty roles, must be licensed RNs in their state, and must pass a national certification exam. Overall, job opportunities for RNs are expected to be good. Generally, those with at least a bachelor's degree in nursing (BSN) will have better job prospects than those without one. Employers may prefer candidates who have some related work experience. For APRNs, overall job opportunities are expected to be excellent. APRNs will be in high demand, particularly in medically underserved areas such as inner cities and rural areas.

OPERATIONS RESEARCH

see Engineering Majors, p. 106.

PEACE STUDIES

see Area Studies, p. 68.

PERSONNEL MANAGEMENT

see Business Majors, p. 77.

PETROLEUM ENGINEERING

see Engineering Majors, p. 110.

PHILOSOPHY

Focuses on ideas and their logical structure, including arguments and investigations about abstract and real phenomena. Includes instruction in logic, ethics, aesthetics, epistemology, metaphysics, symbolism, and history of philosophy, and applications to the theoretical foundations and methods of other disciplines.

Specializations in the Major: Epistemology; esthetics; ethics; history of philosophy; jurisprudence; logic.

Courses Studied in College: Introduction to philosophy; introduction to logic; major thinkers in philosophy; ethical/moral theory; classical philosophy; modern philosophy; contemporary philosophy; seminar (reporting on research). **Usual High School Prerequisites:** Algebra; English; foreign language; social science; history; geometry.

Related Occupations: Philosophy and Religion Teachers, Postsecondary (p. 234).

Career Paths: Philosophy graduates know how to think independently and critically and to write clearly and persuasively. Some find that a philosophy major combines well with further training in law, computer science, or religious studies. With a graduate degree in philosophy, they may teach in college. The bachelor's also can lead to work in various careers that value writing skills, such as journalism, public relations, and advertising. Compared to graduates of more career-oriented majors, these may need to make a greater effort to identify appropriate jobs and convince employers of their qualifications. An undergraduate internship or a minor in a more career-related field would be helpful.

PHYSICAL EDUCATION

see Education Majors, p. 93.

PHYSICS

Focuses on the scientific study of matter and energy and the formulation and testing of the laws governing the behavior of the matter-energy continuum. Includes instruction in classical and modern physics, electricity and magnetism, thermodynamics, mechanics, wave properties, nuclear processes, relativity and quantum theory, quantitative methods, and laboratory methods.

Specializations in the Major: Acoustics; astronomy; biophysics; cosmology; cryophysics; elementary particles; nuclear physics; optics; plasma physics; quantum mechanics; solid-state physics; string theory; theoretical physics.

Courses Studied in College: English composition; introduction to computer science; calculus; differential equations; general chemistry;

mechanics; thermal physics; electricity and magnetism; modern physics; quantum mechanics; advanced experimental physics. **Usual High School Prerequisites:** English; algebra; geometry; trigonometry; chemistry; physics; pre-calculus; computer science; calculus.

Related Occupations: Natural Sciences Managers (p. 227); Physicists (p. 240); Secondary School Teachers, Except Special and Career/Technical Education (p. 251).

Career Paths: Physics is the study of the ways in which various forms of matter and energy interact. Theoretical physicists may study the nature of time or the origin of the universe. Physicists in applied fields may develop new military technologies or new sources of energy. A PhD is needed for most research jobs. Physics PhD holders typically begin their careers in temporary postdoctoral research positions. Expected growth in federal government spending for physics research should increase the need for physicists, especially at colleges and universities and national laboratories.

PLANETARY SCIENCE

see Geology, p. 113.

POLICE SCIENCE

see Criminal Justice, p. 86.

POLITICAL SCIENCE

Focuses on the systematic study of political institutions and behavior. Includes instruction in political philosophy, political theory, comparative government and politics, political parties and interest groups, public opinion, political research methods, studies of the government and politics of specific countries, and studies of specific political institutions and processes. **Also Known As:** Government.

Specializations in the Major: American politics; comparative politics; international relations; political economy; political theory; public administration; public opinion; public policy.

Courses Studied in College: English composition; American government; foreign language; introduction to economics; statistics for business and social sciences; comparative governments; introduction to international relations; political theory; seminar (reporting on research). **Usual High School Prerequisites:** Algebra; English; foreign language; social science; trigonometry; history.

Related Occupations: Managers, All Other (p. 215); Political Scientists (p. 241).

Career Paths: Political science is the study of the origin, development, and operation of political systems. Political scientists research political ideas and analyze governments, policies, political trends, and related issues. Some candidates with a bachelor's degree in political science may find entry-level jobs as research assistants. Many will also find positions outside of politics and policy in fields such as business and law. Candidates with a graduate degree, strong writing and analytical skills, and experience researching or performing policy analysis should have the best job prospects. The federal government employs about half of all political scientists. Others work for organizations that research or advocate for specific causes, such as immigration, health care, or the environment.

PORTUGUESE

see Modern Foreign Language, p. 124.

PRE-AUDIOLOGY

see Pre-Professional Health, p. 131.

PRE-MED

see Pre-Professional Health, p. 131.

PRE-OPTOMETRY

see Pre-Professional Health, p. 131.

PRE-PHARMACY

see Pre-Professional Health, p. 131.

PRE-PROFESSIONAL HEALTH

Prepares individuals for admission to a professional program in a health-care field. **Also Known As:** Pre-Audiology; Pre-Med; Pre-Optometry; Pre-Pharmacy; Pre-Speech Pathology; Pre-Therapy; Pre-Veterinary.

Specializations in the Major: Pre-audiology; pre-med; pre-optometry; pre-pharmacy; pre-speech pathology; pre-therapy; pre-veterinary.

Courses Studied in College: English composition; introduction to psychology; calculus; introduction to sociology; oral communication; general chemistry; general biology; organic chemistry; general physics; human anatomy and physiology; general microbiology; cell biology; genetics; ethics in health care; introduction to medical terminology. **Usual High School Prerequisites:** English; algebra; geometry; trigonometry; pre-calculus; biology; computer science; public speaking; chemistry; foreign language; physics.

Related Occupations: Anesthesiologists (p. 151); Audiologists (p. 156); Chiropractors (p. 163); Dentists, All Other Specialists (p. 183); Dentists, General (p. 183); Family and General Practitioners (p. 190); Internists, General (p. 211); Obstetricians and Gynecologists (p. 228); Occupational Therapists (p. 229); Optometrists (p. 230); Oral and Maxillofacial Surgeons (p. 231); Orthodontists (p. 231); Pediatricians, General (p. 232); Pharmacists (p. 233); Physical Therapists (p. 235); Physician Assistants (p. 235); Physicians and Surgeons, All Other (p. 236); Podiatrists (p. 240); Prosthodontists (p. 244); Psychiatrists (p. 245); Speech-Language Pathologists (p. 259); Surgeons (p. 261); Veterinarians (p. 265).

Career Paths: Professional health careers require a postgraduate professional program, such as chiropractic, dentistry, medical, optometry, pharmacy, podiatry, or veterinary school, or a graduate program in audiology, occupational therapy, physical therapy, physician assisting, or speech/language pathology. Undergraduate entry requirements for the various professional programs vary greatly but usually include several scientific subjects. Many who plan for professional school meet the entry requirements by majoring in an undergraduate program called pre-med, pre-dentistry, etc. Others fill the requirements in a minor while majoring in some other subject. Entrance to postgraduate programs in health care is highly competitive, but there is usually not much attrition of those who are admitted. At that stage, the training includes a lot of hands-on learning in clinical settings. Job opportunities vary among specializations but overall are expected to be good for professional health-care workers. Check the occupational descriptions in chapter 7 for the outlook for specific careers.

PRE-SPEECH PATHOLOGY

see Pre-Professional Health, p. 131.

PRE-THERAPY

see Pre-Professional Health, p. 131.

PRE-VETERINARY

see Pre-Professional Health, p. 131.

PROBABILITY

see Statistics, p. 139.

PSYCHOLOGY

Focuses on the scientific study of individual and collective behavior, the physical and environmental bases of behavior, and the analysis and treatment of behavior problems and disorders. Includes instruction in the principles of the various subfields of psychology, research methods, and psychological assessment and testing methods. **Also Known As:** Behavioral Science.

Specializations in the Major: Behavioral and cellular neuroscience; clinical/counseling; cognitive; developmental; educational; experimental; forensic; industrial/organizational; social; sports.

Courses Studied in College: Introduction to psychology; English composition; statistics; experimental psychology; brain, behavior, and cognition; abnormal psychology; social psychology; psychology of personality; research methods in psychology; seminar (reporting on research). **Usual High School Prerequisites:** Algebra; biology; English; foreign language; social science; trigonometry.

Related Occupations: Clinical, Counseling, and School Psychologists (p. 167); Industrial-Organizational Psychologists (p. 208); Managers, All Other (p. 215); Psychologists, All Other (p. 245).

Career Paths: Psychology is the study of cognitive, emotional, and social processes and human behavior. Psychologists observe, interpret, and record how people relate to one another and their environments. They may gather data in experiments designed to increase knowledge of human behavior, or they may conduct testing or conversations to help people plan their education, work more efficiently, solve interpersonal problems, or overcome destructive behaviors. To analyze data, they need a good command of statistics. Those with a bachelor's degree usually must find employment in another field, such as business administration, sales, or education. A bachelor's degree can also be a good first step toward graduate education in education, law, social work, or another field. A PhD is needed for licensure as a clinical or counseling psychologist. Industrial-organizational psychologists need a master's. School psychologists need an educational specialist degree and may enjoy the best job opportunities in this field. Candidates with a master's degree will face competition for most positions, and many of them will find jobs in a related field outside of psychology.

PUBLIC RELATIONS

Focuses on organizational communication, public relations, and advertising and prepares individuals to function in a wide range of public and private sector positions requiring the skills of persuasive communication. Includes instruction in communications, public relations, and advertising theory; principles and techniques of persuasion; message/image design; marketing strategy; professional writing; public speaking and multi-media presentation skills; digital communications; and applied research.

Specializations in the Major: Creative process; management; new media.

Courses Studied in College: English composition; introduction to economics; introduction to mass media; introduction to advertising; principles of public relations; public relations media; public relations message strategy; public relations writing; media law; news writing and reporting; public relations campaigns; public relations case studies; public opinion; public relations research and planning; organizational communication. **Usual High School Prerequisites:** English; algebra; foreign language; art; literature; public speaking; social science.

Related Occupations: Advertising and Promotions Managers (p. 149); Public Relations and Fundraising Managers (p. 246); Public Relations Specialists (p. 247).

Career Paths: Public relations specialists typically need a bachelor's degree. Entry-level workers typically begin by maintaining files of material about an organization's activities, skimming and retaining relevant media articles, and assembling information for speeches and pamphlets. After gaining experience, public relations specialists begin to write news releases, speeches, and articles for publication, or carry out public relations programs. Positions in public relations management become attainable after many years of experience or perhaps a master's degree. Internships at public relations firms or in the public relations departments of other businesses can be helpful in getting a job as a public relations specialist. Public relations specialists will be needed to respond to news developments and maintain their organization's reputation. Social media are creating new ways for public relations specialists to appeal to consumers and the general public. Because many college graduates apply for the limited amount of public relations positions each year, candidates can expect strong competition for jobs. Candidates can expect particularly strong competition at advertising firms, organizations with large media exposure, and at prestigious public relations firms.

RELIGIOUS STUDIES

Focuses on the nature of religious belief and specific religious and quasi-religious systems. Includes instruction in phenomenology; the sociology, psychology, philosophy, anthropology, literature and art of religion; mythology; scriptural and textual studies; religious history and politics; and specific studies of particular faith communities and their behavior. **Also Known As:** Religion.

Specializations in the Major: Ecumenical studies; history of religion; missionary work; pastoral counseling; pastoral studies; scriptural texts/ language; world religions.

Courses Studied in College: English composition; foreign language; introduction to religious studies; introduction to philosophy; ethical/moral theory; Hebrew Bible; New Testament; non-Western religions; philosophy of religion; history of religion in the West; contemporary theologies; religious ethics. **Usual High School Prerequisites:** Algebra; English; foreign language; social science; history; geometry; public speaking.

Related Occupations: Clergy (p. 166); Directors, Religious Activities and Education (p. 184); Religious Workers, All Other (p. 250).

Career Paths: America was founded largely by religious dissenters and has a continuing devotion to religion. The religious studies major is offered at many colleges, especially those founded by churches. Some graduates feel the call to become professional clergy. The amount of additional education required for ordination varies among religious denominations. Most require several years of seminary training, often following four years of college. Clergy find work in churches, synagogues, and religious schools;

as chaplains for hospitals, prisons, and the military; and as missionaries. Some graduates work as religious educators; some course work in education is helpful background. In addition, many careers in the secular world are options for graduates of religious studies. The program teaches skills in language, literature, critical thinking, and writing that are valuable in journalism, public relations, advertising, and (with an additional degree) law.

RESTAURANT MANAGEMENT

see Business Majors, p. 76.

RISK MANAGEMENT AND INSURANCE

see Business Majors, p. 81.

RUSSIAN

see Modern Foreign Language, p. 124.

SALES MANAGEMENT

see Business Majors, p. 80.

SECONDARY EDUCATION

see Education Majors, p. 94.

SOCIAL WORK

Prepares individuals for the professional practice of social welfare administration and counseling and focuses on the study of organized means of providing basic support services for vulnerable individuals and groups. Includes instruction in social welfare policy; case work planning; social counseling and intervention strategies; administrative procedures and regulations; and specific applications in areas such as child welfare and family services, probation, employment services, and disability counseling.

Specializations in the Major: Advocacy; aging; child welfare; interpersonal violence; health care; mental health; mental retardation; school; substance abuse.

Courses Studied in College: English composition; human growth and development; American government; foreign language; introduction to psychology; introduction to sociology; introduction to economics; statistics for business and social sciences; cultural diversity; human anatomy and physiology; introduction to social welfare; human behavior and the social environment; social work practice with individuals, families, and groups; social welfare policy and issues; field experience/internship; social work research methods; seminar (reporting on research). **Usual High School Prerequisites:** Algebra; trigonometry; biology; English; foreign language; social science; public speaking.

Related Occupations: Child, Family, and School Social Workers (p. 162); Counselors, All Other (p. 180); Health-Care Social Workers (p. 202); Marriage and Family Therapists (p. 219); Mental Health and Substance Abuse Social Workers (p. 225); Probation Officers and Correctional Treatment Specialists (p. 242); Social and Community Service Managers (p. 252); Social Work Teachers, Postsecondary (p. 253); Social Workers, All Other (p. 253).

Career Paths: Social workers help people solve and cope with problems in their everyday lives. Those who do clinical social work also diagnose and treat mental, behavioral, and emotional issues. Social workers are employed in a variety of settings, including mental health clinics, schools, child welfare and human service agencies, hospitals, and private practices. Although most social workers need a bachelor's degree in social work, clinical social workers must have a master's degree and two years of post-master experience in a supervised clinical setting. Clinical social workers must also be licensed in the state in which they practice. Job opportunities are expected to be best in the specializations of substance abuse and mental health.

SOCIOLOGY

Focuses on the systematic study of human social institutions and social relationships. Includes instruction in social theory, sociological research methods, social organization and structure, social stratification and hierarchies, dynamics of social change, family structures, social deviance and control, and applications to the study of specific social groups, social institutions, and social problems. **Also Known As:** Anthropology.

Specializations in the Major: Anthropology; archaeology; comparative criminology; culture and social change; family and marriage; gerontology; human relations; networks and community; population studies; social institutions/organizations; social problems; urban studies.

Courses Studied in College: English composition; introduction to psychology; introduction to sociology; American government; introduction to economics; statistics for business and social sciences; field methods of sociological research; history of social thought; contemporary sociological theory; seminar (reporting on research). **Usual High School Prerequisites:** Algebra; English; foreign language; social science; trigonometry.

Related Occupations: Managers, All Other (p. 215); Sociologists (p. 254).

Career Paths: Sociologists study society and social behavior by examining the groups, cultures, organizations, social institutions, and processes that people develop. Many graduates of bachelor's sociology programs go on to graduate school with the goal of research or teaching. Although some with a bachelor's find work as sociology research assistants, most find positions in other fields, such as social services, administration, management, or sales and marketing. With additional education, they may pursue social work or the law.

SOIL SCIENCE

see Agronomy, p. 66.

SPANISH

see Modern Foreign Language, p. 124.

SPECIAL EDUCATION

see Education Majors, p. 95.

SPEECH STUDIES

see Communication, p. 84.

STATISTICS

Focuses on the relationships between groups of measurements as well as similarities and differences, using probability theory and techniques derived from it. Includes instruction in the principles in probability theory, binomial distribution, regression analysis, standard deviation, stochastic processes, Monte Carlo method, Bayesian statistics, non-parametric statistics, sampling theory, and statistical techniques. **Also Known As:** Probability.

Specializations in the Major: Computer applications; experimental design; mathematical statistics; probability; psychometrics.

Courses Studied in College: Calculus; introduction to computer science; programming in a language (e.g., C, PASCAL, COBOL); introduction to probability; introduction to statistics; linear algebra; stochastic processes; experimental design and analysis; seminar (reporting on research). **Usual High School Prerequisites:** Algebra; geometry; trigonometry; precalculus; calculus; computer science; physics.

Related Occupations: Actuaries (p. 148); Natural Sciences Managers (p. 227); Statisticians (p. 260); Survey Researchers (p. 261).

Career Paths: Even before the explosion of "big data," a large number of fields have relied on making sense from quantitative information recorded by surveys, experiments, checkout counters, or logs of computer activity.

Companies need to analyze this data to improve their business processes, design and develop new products, and advertise products to potential customers. Government agencies also need to analyze data to gauge the impact of policies. Graduates of statistics programs bring valuable skills to these tasks. Job candidates with course work or experience in a related discipline—such as computer science, engineering, physics, mathematics, or finance—are particularly desirable to many employers. Graduates with a bachelor's may find work as trainee actuaries or as research assistants; usually a master's is required to work as a statistician. Research and academic jobs generally require a PhD. Job prospects for statisticians are projected to be very good. An increasing number of jobs over the next decade will require high levels of statistical knowledge. Job opportunities for statisticians are expected to be favorable for those with very strong quantitative and data analysis skills. Actuaries should expect strong competition for jobs. Actuaries make up a small occupation, and the relatively high pay and comfortable working conditions make being an actuary a desirable career. Students who have passed at least two actuarial exams and have had an internship while in college should have the best job prospects for entry-level positions.

STUDIO ART

Prepares individuals to generally function as creative artists in the visual and plastic media. Includes instruction in the traditional fine arts media (drawing, painting, sculpture, printmaking, CAD/CAM) or also modern media (ceramics, textiles, intermedia, photography, digital images), theory of art, color theory, composition and perspective, anatomy, the techniques and procedures for maintaining equipment and managing a studio, and art portfolio marketing. **Also Known As:** Fine Art.

Specializations in the Major: Art education; ceramics; crafts; painting; screenprinting; sculpture; studio art.

Courses Studied in College: Basic drawing; art history: prehistoric to Renaissance; art history: Renaissance to modern; figure drawing; introduction to visual design; digital art; a medium (e.g., painting, sculpture, ceramics); art practicum. **Usual High School Prerequisites:** English; foreign language; literature; history; art.

Related Occupations: Artists and Related Workers, All Other (p. 155); Craft Artists (p. 180); Fine Artists, Including Painters, Sculptors, and Illustrators (p. 195).

Career Paths: Competition for jobs as craft and fine artists is expected to be strong, because there are more qualified candidates than available jobs. Only the most successful craft and fine artists receive major commissions for their work. Talented individuals who have developed a mastery of artistic techniques and marketing skills will have the best job prospects. Some graduates work in commercial media such as illustration or cartooning. Many other graduates teach privately or in public schools or colleges. College teaching requires a master's degree.

TECHNOLOGY EDUCATION

see Education Majors, p. 97.

THEATER ARTS

Focuses on the general study of dramatic works and their performance. Includes instruction in major works of dramatic literature, dramatic styles and types, and the principles of organizing and producing full live or filmed productions. **Also Known As:** Drama.

Specializations in the Major: Acting; design and technology; directing; musical theater; writing for the stage and media.

Courses Studied in College: History of theater; dramatic literature; acting technique; directing technique; theater technology (e.g., set, costume, lighting); theater practicum. **Usual High School Prerequisites:** English; foreign language; literature; public speaking.

Related Occupations: Actors (p. 148); Entertainers and Performers, Sports and Related Workers, All Other (p. 188); Producers and Directors (p. 242).

Career Paths: The ancient art form of drama now provides job opportunities in several media, from the stage to the computer screen. As in other performing arts, opportunities are better for teachers than for performers and directors. Teaching at the postsecondary level usually requires a master's degree. With experience, some actors find work as directors. Nonperformers who hold this degree may also find jobs in the technical aspects of theater and video production: set design, lighting, costume design, and makeup. Student performances supplement classroom work.

WOMEN'S STUDIES

see Area Studies, p. 68.

ZOOLOGY

see Biology, p. 71.

KEY POINTS OF CHAPTER 6

❱ Of the majors described in this chapter, one or more probably seem like a good fit for you.

❱ When you consider a major, think about the whole package: what you'd study for four years, what you'd need in your background from high school, what specializations may be open to you, and what careers it might lead to.

❱ The careers linked to these majors are not the only options for graduates. With an additional degree or on-the-job training, other careers become possibilities.

CHAPTER 7

DESCRIPTIONS OF RELATED OCCUPATIONS

The 161 occupations and 100 job specializations in this chapter are common career paths for people who get bachelor's degrees in one of the 61 college majors covered by this book. You probably want to start by looking at occupations related to the majors you explored in chapter 6. However, you may browse other occupations that arouse your curiosity. I'm sure there are some here that you've never heard of before. Other occupations may be familiar, but you may not have thought about what you'd need to study for career entry.

The occupations are ordered alphabetically by title. If there's an occupation that you look for and can't find, look in the index. It may be cross-referenced there under an alternate title. (Many occupations are excluded because college is not the usual entry route.)

The facts for the occupations are derived from the U.S. Department of Labor and are based on the most recent data available. Understand that the descriptions are generalizations that sometimes cover several specializations. Also, the figures here are national averages. Earnings and job outlook vary in different geographical regions and job specializations.

Although you may be in a hurry now, make plans to get more detailed and more locally-specific information about any occupation that you're considering as a career goal.

Here's the information you'll find for each occupation:

- **Title and definition.** The titles, which order the occupations alphabetically, are derived from the Standard Occupational Classification (SOC). SOC is used by all departments of the U.S. government that provide information about careers. Some occupations also include the titles and information for **job specializations**; these titles are taken from the more-specific O*NET database. Many of the following topics of information are available only at the SOC level.
- **Annual Earnings:**
  - **Average.** This figure is an estimate of the median earnings for the occupation; half of the workers earn more, half less. It applies to May 2013, but in this time of low inflation, it remains very relevant for several years.
  - **Middle 50%.** This range also applies to May 2013. If you know that earnings for various careers in your community tend to be higher or lower than the national average, this set of figures may be more useful to you than the average.
- **Employment Outlook:**
  - **Workforce, 2012.** This figure tells you how many wage- and salary-earners were working in the occupation. You need to keep this figure in mind when you consider the next two figures.
  - **Projected Growth.** This figure is the best estimate by the Bureau of Labor Statistic of how much the workforce of the occupation will grow between 2012 and 2022. Understand that this is an average over a 10-year period; changes in the economy will probably speed up and slow down growth at various times.
  - **Projected Annual Openings.** This figure covers job openings from both job growth and worker turnover—that is, replacement of workers who quit or die. Job opportunities are likely to be very good for occupations that have a large workforce and are growing

fast. Conversely, occupations with a very large workforce may offer good job opportunities through turnover even if they are not growing. This figure also is an average and will vary as the economy experiences upswings and downturns.

) **Personality Type(s).** Here are listed the primary and secondary personality types for the occupation. If the names are not meaningful to you, consult the definitions in the appendix.

) **Top Skills.** These skills are listed in descending order of the level required for the occupation. To see the specific skills listed under these large skill categories, consult the appendix. For a few occupations, skill data is not available.

) **Work Environment.** These characteristics of the work setting are those for which the rating in O*NET exceeds the average for all occupations. The order of the characteristics does not indicate their importance. Note that when workplace hazards are present, workers are given appropriate equipment and training.

) **Typical Entry Requirements:**

) **Education.** Check here to see whether the occupation typically requires more or less education than a bachelor's degree. About two dozen occupations here actually require less education, but the bachelor's may be an advantage in the job market. About three dozen occupations here require a master's, doctoral, or professional degree; the information here indicates what field of study is usually required.

) **Work Experience.** Of the occupations in this chapter, 35 typically require some work experience in a related occupation. Many of these are managerial positions that workers qualify for after getting a thorough background in the industry. In a few cases, it may be possible to substitute a postgraduate degree for this entry-level work experience.

) **On-the-Job Training.** Of the occupations in this chapter, 56 typically require entry-level workers to get on-the-job training before they become fully qualified. This includes student teaching for public school educators and internships for many health-care occupations.

❯ Related Majors. These are the majors that are typically completed by people who want to enter this occupation. Understand that graduates of other majors may sometimes find employment in the occupation.

ACCOUNTANTS AND AUDITORS

Examine, analyze, and interpret accounting records to prepare financial statements, give advice, or audit and evaluate statements prepared by others. Install or advise on systems of recording costs or other financial and budgetary data.

Annual Earnings. Average: $65,080. **Middle 50%:** $50,340–$86,130.

Employment Outlook. Workforce 2012: 1,275,400. **Projected Growth 2012–22:** 13.1%. **Projected Annual Openings:** 54,420.

Typical Entry Requirements. Education: Bachelor's degree. **Work Experience:** None. **On-the-Job Training:** None.

Related Majors: Accounting, p. 73.

JOB SPECIALIZATION: ACCOUNTANTS

Analyze financial information and prepare financial reports to determine or maintain record of assets, liabilities, profit and loss, tax liability, or other financial activities within an organization.

Personality Type(s): Conventional–Enterprising. **Top Skills:** Mathematics; Social; Thought-Processing; Management; Communication; Science. **Work Environment:** Indoors; sitting; repetitive motions.

JOB SPECIALIZATION: AUDITORS

Examine and analyze accounting records to determine financial status of establishment and prepare financial reports concerning operating procedures.

Personality Type(s): Conventional–Enterprising–Investigative. **Top Skills:** Mathematics; Thought-Processing; Social; Management; Communication; Science. **Work Environment:** Indoors; sitting.

ACTORS

Play parts in stage, television, radio, video, motion picture productions, or other settings for entertainment, information, or instruction. Interpret serious or comic role by speech, gesture, and body movement to entertain or inform audience. May dance and sing.

Annual Earnings. Average: No data available. **Middle 50%:** No data available.

Employment Outlook. Workforce 2012: 79,800. **Projected Growth 2012–22:** 4.1%. **Projected Annual Openings:** 2,890.

Personality Type(s): Artistic–Enterprising. **Top Skills:** Social; Communication. **Work Environment:** Indoors; standing.

Typical Entry Requirements. Education: Some college, no degree. **Work Experience: None. On-the-Job Training:** Long-term on-the-job training.

Related Majors: Theater Arts, p. 141.

ACTUARIES

Analyze statistical data, such as mortality, accident, sickness, disability, and retirement rates and construct probability tables to forecast risk and liability for payment of future benefits. May ascertain insurance rates required and cash reserves necessary to ensure payment of future benefits.

Annual Earnings. Average: $94,340. **Middle 50%:** $71,000–$132,490.

Employment Outlook. Workforce 2012: 24,300. **Projected Growth 2012–22:** 26.1%. **Projected Annual Openings:** 1,320.

Personality Type(s): Conventional–Investigative–Enterprising. **Top Skills:** Mathematics; Thought-Processing; Technology/Programming; Social; Management; Communication; Science. **Work Environment:** Indoors; sitting.

Typical Entry Requirements. Education: Bachelor's degree. **Work Experience:** None. **On-the-Job Training:** Long-term on-the-job training.

Related Majors: Actuarial Science, p. 64; Statistics, p. 139.

ADMINISTRATIVE SERVICES MANAGERS

Plan, direct, or coordinate one or more administrative services of an organization, such as records and information management, mail distribution, facilities planning and maintenance, custodial operations, and other office support services.

Annual Earnings. Average: $82,310. **Middle 50%:** $61,200–$110,500.

Employment Outlook. Workforce 2012: 280,800. **Projected Growth 2012–22:** 12.2%. **Projected Annual Openings**: 7,990.

Personality Type(s): Enterprising–Conventional. **Top Skills:** Management; Social; Communication; Thought-Processing. **Work Environment:** Indoors; sitting.

Typical Entry Requirements. Education: Bachelor's degree. **Work Experience:** Less than 5 years. **On-the-Job Training:** None.

Related Majors: Business Management and Administration, p. 74.

ADVERTISING AND PROMOTIONS MANAGERS

Plan, direct, or coordinate advertising policies and programs or produce collateral materials, such as posters, contests, coupons, or give-aways, to create extra interest in the purchase of a product or service for a department, an entire organization, or on an account basis.

Annual Earnings. Average: $93,880. **Middle 50%:** $64,370–$145,250.

Employment Outlook. Workforce 2012: 35,500. **Projected Growth 2012–22:** 6.9%. **Projected Annual Openings:** 1,340.

Personality Type(s): Enterprising–Artistic–Conventional. **Top Skills:** Management; Social; Thought-Processing; Mathematics; Communication. **Work Environment:** Indoors; sitting.

Typical Entry Requirements. Education: Bachelor's degree. **Work Experience:** Less than 5 years. **On-the-Job Training:** None.

Related Majors: Marketing, p. 80; Public Relations, p. 134.

JOB SPECIALIZATION: GREEN MARKETERS

Create and implement methods to market green products and services.

Personality Type(s): Enterprising–Artistic–Investigative. **Top Skills:** No data available. **Work Environment:** No data available.

AEROSPACE ENGINEERS

Perform engineering duties in designing, constructing, and testing aircraft, missiles, and spacecraft. May conduct basic and applied research to evaluate adaptability of materials and equipment to aircraft design and manufacture. May recommend improvements in testing equipment and techniques.

Annual Earnings. Average: $103,870. **Middle 50%:** $81,710–$127,740.

Employment Outlook. Workforce 2012: 83,000. **Projected Growth 2012–22:** 7.3%. **Projected Annual Openings:** 2,540.

Personality Type(s): Investigative–Realistic. **Top Skills:** Science; Technology/Programming; Thought-Processing; Mathematics; Social; Communication; Installation; Management. **Work Environment:** Indoors; sitting.

Typical Entry Requirements. Education: Bachelor's degree. **Work Experience:** None. **On-the-Job Training:** None.

Related Majors: Aeronautical/Aerospace Engineering, p. 98; Electrical Engineering, p. 105; Mechanical Engineering, p. 107.

AGRICULTURAL ENGINEERS

Apply knowledge of engineering technology and biological science to agricultural problems concerned with power and machinery, electrification, structures, soil and water conservation, and processing of agricultural products.

Annual Earnings. Average: $74,450. **Middle 50%:** $61,910–$94,020.

Employment Outlook. Workforce 2012: 2,600. **Projected Growth 2012– 22:** 4.8%. **Projected Annual Openings**: 80.

Personality Type(s): Investigative–Realistic–Enterprising. **Top Skills:** Mathematics; Technology/Programming; Science; Thought-Processing; Social; Management; Equipment Use/Maintenance; Communication. **Work Environment:** Indoors; outdoors; sitting.

Typical Entry Requirements. Education: Bachelor's degree. **Work Experience:** None. **On-the-Job Training:** None.

Related Majors: Agricultural Engineering, p. 99.

ANESTHESIOLOGISTS

Physicians who administer anesthetics prior to, during, or after surgery or other medical procedures.

Annual Earnings. Average: No data available. **Middle 50%:** No data available.

Employment Outlook. Workforce 2012: 33,900. **Projected Growth 2012–22:** 24.4%. **Projected Annual Openings**: 1,670.

Personality Type(s): Investigative–Realistic–Social. **Top Skills:** Science; Equipment Use/Maintenance; Management; Mathematics; Social; Technology/Programming; Thought-Processing; Communication. **Work Environment:** Indoors; sitting; standing; using hands; noisy; contaminants; radiation; disease or infections.

Typical Entry Requirements. Education: Professional degree (in Medicine). **Work Experience:** None. **On-the-Job Training:** Internship/residency.

Related Majors: Pre-Professional Health (or any major, plus courses required for entry to medical school), p. 131.

ARCHITECTS, EXCEPT LANDSCAPE AND NAVAL

Plan and design structures, such as private residences, office buildings, theaters, factories, and other structural property.

Annual Earnings. Average: $74,110. **Middle 50%:** $57,620–$94,120.

Employment Outlook. Workforce 2012: 107,400. **Projected Growth 2012–22:** 17.3%. **Projected Annual Openings**: 4,410.

Personality Type(s): Artistic–Investigative. **Top Skills:** Science; Thought-Processing; Technology/Programming; Management; Mathematics; Social; Communication. **Work Environment:** Indoors; sitting; using hands; repetitive motions.

Typical Entry Requirements. Education: Five-year bachelor's degree. **Work Experience:** None. **On-the-Job Training:** Internship.

Related Majors: Architecture, p. 67.

ARCHITECTURAL AND ENGINEERING MANAGERS

Plan, direct, or coordinate activities in such fields as architecture and engineering or research and development in these fields.

Annual Earnings. Average: $128,170. **Middle 50%:** $102,160–$159,830.

Employment Outlook. Workforce 2012: 193,800. **Projected Growth 2012–22:** 6.7%. **Projected Annual Openings:** 6,060.

Personality Type(s): Enterprising–Realistic–Investigative. **Top Skills:** Mathematics; Management; Science; Thought-Processing; Technology/Programming; Communication; Installation; Social. **Work Environment:** Indoors; sitting.

Typical Entry Requirements. Education: Bachelor's degree. **Work Experience:** 5 years or more. **On-the-Job Training:** None.

Related Majors: Aeronautical/Aerospace Engineering, p. 98; Agricultural Engineering, p. 99; Architecture, p. 67; Bioengineering, p. 100; Chemical Engineering, p. 102; Civil Engineering, p. 103; Computer Engineering, p. 104; Electrical Engineering, p. 105; Industrial Engineering, p. 106; Landscape Architecture, p. 120; Mechanical Engineering, p. 107; Metallurgical Engineering, p. 108; Petroleum Engineering, p. 110.

JOB SPECIALIZATION: BIOFUELS/BIODIESEL TECHNOLOGY AND PRODUCT DEVELOPMENT MANAGERS

Define, plan, or execute biofuels/biodiesel research programs that evaluate alternative feedstock and process technologies with near-term commercial potential.

Personality Type(s): Enterprising–Investigative. **Top Skills:** Science; Thought-Processing; Social; Mathematics; Management; Equipment Use/Maintenance; Communication; Technology/Programming. **Work Environment:** Indoors; sitting; contaminants; hazardous conditions.

ARCHIVISTS

Appraise, edit, and direct safekeeping of permanent records and historically valuable documents. Participate in research activities based on archival materials.

Annual Earnings. Average: $49,110. **Middle 50%:** $37,550–$64,550.

Employment Outlook. Workforce 2012: 6,500. **Projected Growth 2012–22:** 16.6%. **Projected Annual Openings**: 250.

Personality Type(s): Conventional–Investigative. **Top Skills:** Management; Communication; Thought-Processing; Social. **Work Environment:** Indoors; sitting.

Typical Entry Requirements. Education: Master's degree (in History, Library Science, Archival Science, or Records Management). **Work Experience:** None. **On-the-Job Training:** None.

Related Majors: Art History, p. 69; History, p. 117.

AREA, ETHNIC, AND CULTURAL STUDIES TEACHERS, POSTSECONDARY

Teach courses pertaining to the culture and development of an area, an ethnic group, or any other group, such as Latin American studies, women's studies, or urban affairs. Includes both teachers primarily engaged in teaching and those who do a combination of teaching and research.

Annual Earnings. Average: $66,770. **Middle 50%:** $49,660–$92,810.

Employment Outlook. Workforce 2012: 12,400. **Projected Growth 2012–22:** 15.8%. **Projected Annual Openings**: 380.

Personality Type(s): Social–Investigative–Artistic. **Top Skills:** Science; Communication; Thought-Processing; Social. **Work Environment:** Indoors; sitting.

Typical Entry Requirements. Education: Doctoral degree (in an Area Studies specialization). **Work Experience:** None. **On-the-Job Training:** None.

Related Majors: Area Studies, p. 68.

ART DIRECTORS

Formulate design concepts and presentation approaches for visual communications media, such as print, broadcasting, and advertising. Direct workers engaged in art work or layout design.

Annual Earnings. Average: $83,000. **Middle 50%:** $58,950–$120,190.

Employment Outlook. Workforce 2012: 74,800. **Projected Growth 2012–22:** 3.0%. **Projected Annual Openings:** 2,000.

Personality Type(s): Artistic–Enterprising. **Top Skills:** Management; Technology/Programming; Thought-Processing; Social; Communication; Mathematics. **Work Environment:** Indoors; sitting; using hands; repetitive motions.

Typical Entry Requirements. Education: Bachelor's degree. **Work Experience:** 5 years or more. **On-the-Job Training:** None.

Related Majors: Graphic Design, p. 114.

ARTISTS AND RELATED WORKERS, ALL OTHER

All artists and related workers not listed separately.

Annual Earnings. Average: $53,720. **Middle 50%:** $34,020–$82,350.

Employment Outlook. Workforce 2012: 11,400. **Projected Growth 2012–22:** -1.5%. **Projected Annual Openings:** 270.

Typical Entry Requirements. Education: High school diploma or equivalent. **Work Experience:** None. **On-the-Job Training:** Long-term on-the-job training.

Related Majors: Graphic Design, p. 114; Studio Art, p. 140.

AUDIOLOGISTS

Assess and treat persons with hearing and related disorders. May fit hearing aids and provide auditory training. May perform research related to hearing problems.

Annual Earnings. Average: $71,170. **Middle 50%:** $57,800–$87,300.

Employment Outlook. Workforce 2012: 13,000. **Projected Growth 2012–22:** 33.6%. **Projected Annual Openings:** 700.

Personality Type(s): Investigative–Social. **Top Skills:** Science; Thought-Processing; Social; Mathematics; Management; Installation; Equipment Use/Maintenance; Communication; Technology/Programming. **Work Environment:** Indoors; sitting; using hands; disease or infections.

Typical Entry Requirements. Education: Professional degree (in Audiology). **Work Experience:** None. **On-the-Job Training:** None.

Related Majors: Pre-Professional Health (or any major, plus courses required for entry to graduate program in audiology), p. 131.

BIOLOGICAL SCIENTISTS, ALL OTHER

All biological scientists not listed separately.

Annual Earnings. Average: $72,720. **Middle 50%:** $54,710–$87,260.

Employment Outlook. Workforce 2012: 34,300. **Projected Growth 2012–22:** -0.6%. **Projected Annual Openings:** 980.

Typical Entry Requirements. Education: Bachelor's degree. **Work Experience:** None. **On-the-Job Training:** None.

Related Majors: Biology, p. 71.

JOB SPECIALIZATION: BIOINFORMATICS SCIENTISTS

Conduct research using bioinformatics theory and methods in areas such as pharmaceuticals, medical technology, biotechnology, computational biology, proteomics, computer information science, biology and medical informatics. May design databases and develop algorithms for processing and analyzing genomic information, or other biological information.

Personality Type(s): Investigative–Conventional–Realistic. **Top Skills:** Science; Technology/Programming; Mathematics; Communication; Management; Thought-Processing; Social. **Work Environment:** Indoors; sitting.

JOB SPECIALIZATION: GENETICISTS

Research and study the inheritance of traits at the molecular, organism or population level. May evaluate or treat patients with genetic disorders.

Personality Type(s): Investigative–Artistic–Realistic. **Top Skills:** Science; Mathematics; Social; Communication; Management; Technology/Programming; Thought-Processing. **Work Environment:** Indoors; sitting; using hands.

JOB SPECIALIZATION: MOLECULAR AND CELLULAR BIOLOGISTS

Research and study cellular molecules and organelles to understand cell function and organization.

Personality Type(s): Investigative–Realistic–Artistic. **Top Skills:** Science; Mathematics; Communication; Technology/Programming; Thought-Processing; Management; Social; Equipment Use/Maintenance. **Work Environment:** Indoors; sitting; using hands; hazardous conditions.

BIOMEDICAL ENGINEERS

Apply knowledge of engineering, biology, and biomechanical principles to the design, development, and evaluation of biological and health systems and products, such as artificial organs, prostheses, instrumentation, medical information systems, and health management and care delivery systems.

Annual Earnings. Average: $88,670. **Middle 50%:** $68,720–$113,250.

Employment Outlook. Workforce 2012: 19,400. **Projected Growth 2012–22:** 26.6%. **Projected Annual Openings:** 1,010.

Personality Type(s): Investigative–Realistic. **Top Skills:** Science; Technology/Programming; Mathematics; Installation; Equipment Use/ Maintenance; Communication; Thought-Processing; Management; Social. **Work Environment:** Indoors; sitting.

Typical Entry Requirements. Education: Bachelor's degree. **Work Experience:** None. **On-the-Job Training:** None.

Related Majors: Bioengineering, p. 100.

BROADCAST NEWS ANALYSTS

Analyze, interpret, and broadcast news received from various sources.

Annual Earnings. Average: $60,470. **Middle 50%:** $37,890–$104,670.

Employment Outlook. Workforce 2012: 5,900. **Projected Growth 2012–22:** -2.3%. **Projected Annual Openings:** 200.

Personality Type(s): Artistic–Social–Enterprising. **Top Skills:** Communication; Thought-Processing; Social. **Work Environment:** Indoors; sitting; repetitive motions; noisy.

Typical Entry Requirements. Education: Bachelor's degree. **Work Experience:** None. **On-the-Job Training:** None.

Related Majors: Journalism, p. 119.

BUDGET ANALYSTS

Examine budget estimates for completeness, accuracy, and conformance with procedures and regulations. Analyze budgeting and accounting reports.

Annual Earnings. Average: $70,110. **Middle 50%:** $56,020–$87,630.

Employment Outlook. Workforce 2012: 61,700. **Projected Growth 2012–22:** 6.1%. **Projected Annual Openings**: 2,850.

Personality Type(s): Conventional–Enterprising–Investigative. **Top Skills:** Mathematics; Thought-Processing; Management; Communication. **Work Environment:** Indoors; sitting; repetitive motions.

Typical Entry Requirements. Education: Bachelor's degree. **Work Experience:** None. **On-the-Job Training:** None.

Related Majors: Accounting, p. 73; Finance, p. 75.

CAREER/TECHNICAL EDUCATION TEACHERS, MIDDLE SCHOOL

Teach occupational, career and technical, or vocational subjects in public or private schools at the middle, intermediate, or junior high level, which falls between elementary and senior high school as defined by applicable laws and regulations.

Annual Earnings. Average: $54,270. **Middle 50%:** $44,330–$67,120.

Employment Outlook. Workforce 2012: 18,200. **Projected Growth 2012–22:** 5.2%. **Projected Annual Openings**: 490.

Personality Type(s): Social–Artistic–Conventional. **Top Skills:** Management; Social; Science; Communication; Thought-Processing. **Work Environment:** Indoors; standing; walking and running; using hands; noisy; contaminants.

Typical Entry Requirements. Education: Bachelor's degree. **Work Experience:** Less than 5 years. **On-the-Job Training:** Student teaching.

Related Majors: Business Education, p. 89; Family and Consumer Sciences Education, p. 92; Technology Education (see your state's requirements), p. 97.

CAREER/TECHNICAL EDUCATION TEACHERS, SECONDARY SCHOOL

Teach occupational, career and technical, or vocational subjects at the secondary school level in public or private schools.

Annual Earnings. Average: $55,120. **Middle 50%:** $45,110–$67,840.

Employment Outlook. Workforce 2012: 85,400. **Projected Growth 2012–22:** 5.0%. **Projected Annual Openings**: 2,750.

Personality Type(s): Social. **Top Skills:** Management; Technology/Programming; Social; Mathematics; Thought-Processing; Communication. **Work Environment:** Indoors; standing; walking and running; using hands; noisy; contaminants.

Typical Entry Requirements. Education: Bachelor's degree. **Work Experience:** Less than 5 years. **On-the-Job Training:** Student teaching.

Related Majors: Business Education, p. 89; Family and Consumer Sciences Education, p. 92; Technology Education (see your state's requirements), p. 97.

CHEMICAL ENGINEERS

Design chemical plant equipment and devise processes for manufacturing chemicals and products, such as gasoline, synthetic rubber, plastics, detergents, cement, paper, and pulp, by applying principles and technology of chemistry, physics, and engineering.

Annual Earnings. Average: $95,730. **Middle 50%:** $74,870–$121,250.

Employment Outlook. Workforce 2012: 33,300. **Projected Growth 2012–22:** 4.5%. **Projected Annual Openings**: 920.

Personality Type(s): Investigative–Realistic. **Top Skills:** Science; Mathematics; Technology/Programming; Thought-Processing; Management; Social; Equipment Use/Maintenance; Communication. **Work Environment:** Indoors; sitting.

Typical Entry Requirements. Education: Bachelor's degree. **Work Experience:** None. **On-the-Job Training:** None.

Related Majors: Chemical Engineering, p. 102.

CHEMISTS

Conduct qualitative and quantitative chemical analyses or experiments in laboratories for quality or process control or to develop new products or knowledge.

Annual Earnings. Average: $72,350. **Middle 50%:** $52,850–$97,100.

Employment Outlook. Workforce 2012: 87,900. **Projected Growth 2012–22:** 5.6%. **Projected Annual Openings**: 2,780.

Personality Type(s): Investigative–Realistic–Conventional. **Top Skills:** Science; Mathematics; Equipment Use/Maintenance; Management; Communication; Technology/Programming; Thought-Processing. **Work Environment:** Indoors; sitting; using hands; noisy; contaminants; hazardous conditions.

Typical Entry Requirements. Education: Bachelor's degree. **Work Experience:** None. **On-the-Job Training:** None.

Related Majors: Chemistry, p. 83.

CHIEF EXECUTIVES

Determine and formulate policies and provide overall direction of companies or private and public sector organizations within guidelines set up by a board of directors or similar governing body. Plan, direct, or coordinate operational activities at the highest level of management with the help of subordinate executives and staff managers.

Annual Earnings. Average: $171,610. **Middle 50%:** $110,610–$187,200+.

Eployment Outlook. Workforce 2012: 330,500. **Projected Growth 2012–22:** 5.3%. **Projected Annual Openings:** 8,780.

Personality Type(s): Enterprising–Conventional. **Top Skills:** Management; Thought-Processing; Mathematics; Social; Communication. **Work Environment:** Indoors; sitting.

Typical Entry Requirements. Education: Bachelor's degree. **Work Experience:** 5 years or more. **On-the-Job Training:** None.

Related Majors: Business Management and Administration, p. 74; Finance, p. 75.

JOB SPECIALIZATION: CHIEF SUSTAINABILITY OFFICERS

Communicate and coordinate with management, shareholders, customers, and employees to address sustainability issues. Enact or oversee a corporate sustainability strategy.

Personality Type(s): Enterprising–Conventional–Investigative. **Top Skills:** Management; Social; Thought-Processing; Technology/Programming; Communication; Mathematics. **Work Environment:** Indoors; sitting.

CHILD, FAMILY, AND SCHOOL SOCIAL WORKERS

Provide social services and assistance to improve the social and psychological functioning of children and their families and to maximize the family well-being and the academic functioning of children. May assist parents, arrange adoptions, and find foster homes for abandoned or abused children. In schools, they address such problems as teenage pregnancy, misbehavior, and truancy. May also advise teachers.

Annual Earnings. Average: $42,120. **Middle 50%:** $33,610–$55,320.

Employment Outlook. Workforce 2012: 285,700. **Projected Growth 2012–22:** 15.1%. **Projected Annual Openings**: 10,360.

Personality Type(s): Social–Enterprising. **Top Skills:** Science; Social; Communication; Thought-Processing; Management. **Work Environment:** Indoors; sitting.

Typical Entry Requirements. Education: Bachelor's degree. **Work Experience:** None. **On-the-Job Training:** None.

Related Majors: Social Work (or any major, plus courses required for entry to master's program in social work), p. 136.

CHIROPRACTORS

Assess, treat, and care for patients by manipulation of spine and musculoskeletal system. May provide spinal adjustment or address sacral or pelvic misalignment.

Annual Earnings. Average: $65,300. **Middle 50%:** $44,640–$95,070.

Employment Outlook. Workforce 2012: 44,400. **Projected Growth 2012–22:** 14.6%. **Projected Annual Openings**: 1,520.

Personality Type(s): Social–Investigative–Realistic. **Top Skills:** Science; Social; Thought-Processing; Communication; Management. **Work Environment:** Indoors; standing; using hands; bending or twisting body; repetitive motions; disease or infections.

Typical Entry Requirements. Education: Professional degree (in Chiropractic). **Work Experience:** None. **On-the-Job Training:** None.

Related Majors: Pre-Professional Health (or any major, plus courses required for entry to chiropractic school), p. 131.

CHOREOGRAPHERS

Create new dance routines. Rehearse performance of routines. May direct and stage presentations.

Annual Earnings. Average: $44,130. **Middle 50%:** $28,510–$65,850.

Employment Outlook. Workforce 2012: 10,200. **Projected Growth 2012–22:** 24.3%. **Projected Annual Openings**: 540.

Personality Type(s): Artistic–Social–Enterprising. **Top Skills:** Social; Management; Thought-Processing. **Work Environment:** Indoors; standing; walking and running; kneeling, crouching, stooping, or crawling; balancing; bending or twisting body; repetitive motions.

Typical Entry Requirements. Education: High school diploma or equivalent. **Work Experience:** 5 years or more. **On-the-Job Training:** Long-term on-the-job training.

Related Majors: Dance, p. 87.

CIVIL ENGINEERS

Perform engineering duties in planning, designing, and overseeing construction and maintenance of building structures, and facilities, such as roads, railroads, airports, bridges, harbors, channels, dams, irrigation projects, pipelines, power plants, and water and sewage systems. Includes architectural, structural, traffic, ocean, and geo-technical engineers.

Annual Earnings. Average: $80,770. **Middle 50%:** $63,850–$101,660.

Employment Outlook. Workforce 2012: 272,900. **Projected Growth 2012–22:** 19.7%. **Projected Annual Openings**: 12,010.

Personality Type(s): Realistic–Investigative–Conventional. **Top Skills:** Science; Mathematics; Thought-Processing; Technology/Programming; Management; Social; Communication. **Work Environment:** Indoors; outdoors; sitting; noisy.

Typical Entry Requirements. Education: Bachelor's degree. **Work Experience:** None. **On-the-Job Training:** None.

Related Majors: Civil Engineering, p. 103.

JOB SPECIALIZATION: TRANSPORTATION ENGINEERS

Develop plans for surface transportation projects, according to established engineering standards and state or federal construction policy. Prepare designs, specifications, or estimates for transportation facilities. Plan modifications of existing streets, highways, or freeways to improve traffic flow.

Personality Type(s): Realistic–Investigative. **Top Skills:** Management; Technology/Programming; Mathematics; Science; Social; Communication; Thought-Processing. **Work Environment:** Indoors; sitting.

CLAIMS ADJUSTERS, EXAMINERS, AND INVESTIGATORS

Review settled claims to determine that payments and settlements are made in accordance with company practices and procedures. Confer with legal counsel on claims requiring litigation. May also settle insurance claims.

Annual Earnings. Average: $61,190. **Middle 50%:** $46,530–$75,380.

Employment Outlook. Workforce 2012: 297,600. **Projected Growth 2012–22:** 3.9%. **Projected Annual Openings:** 8,030.

Typical Entry Requirements. Education: High school diploma or equivalent. **Work Experience:** None. **On-the-Job Training:** Long-term on-the-job training.

Related Majors: Risk Management and Insurance, p. 81.

JOB SPECIALIZATION: CLAIMS EXAMINERS, PROPERTY AND CASUALTY INSURANCE

Review settled insurance claims to determine that payments and settlements have been made in accordance with company practices and procedures. Report overpayments, underpayments, and other irregularities. Confer with legal counsel on claims requiring litigation.

Personality Type(s): Conventional–Enterprising. **Top Skills:** Mathematics; Social; Communication. **Work Environment:** Indoors; sitting; repetitive motions; noisy.

JOB SPECIALIZATION: INSURANCE ADJUSTERS, EXAMINERS, AND INVESTIGATORS

Investigate, analyze, and determine the extent of insurance company's liability concerning personal, casualty, or property loss or damages, and attempt to effect settlement with claimants. Correspond with or interview medical specialists, agents, witnesses, or claimants to compile information. Calculate benefit payments and approve payment of claims within a certain monetary limit.

Personality Type(s): Conventional–Enterprising. **Top Skills:** Management; Social; Mathematics; Communication. **Work Environment:** Indoors; sitting; repetitive motions.

CLERGY

Conduct religious worship and perform other spiritual functions associated with beliefs and practices of religious faith or denomination. Provide spiritual and moral guidance and assistance to members.

Annual Earnings. Average: $43,800. **Middle 50%:** $31,190–$58,310.

Employment Outlook. Workforce 2012: 239,600. **Projected Growth 2012–22:** 9.8%. **Projected Annual Openings:** 7,260.

Personality Type(s): Social–Enterprising–Artistic. **Top Skills:** Management; Social; Communication; Mathematics; Thought-Processing. **Work Environment:** Indoors; sitting.

Typical Entry Requirements. Education: Bachelor's degree (higher for many denominations). **Work Experience:** None. **On-the-Job Training:** Moderate-term on-the-job training.

Related Majors: Religious Studies, p. 135.

CLINICAL, COUNSELING, AND SCHOOL PSYCHOLOGISTS

Diagnose and treat mental disorders; learning disabilities; and cognitive, behavioral, and emotional problems, using individual, child, family, and group therapies. May design and implement behavior modification programs.

Annual Earnings. Average: $67,760. **Middle 50%:** $50,700–$88,650.

Employment Outlook. Workforce 2012: 145,100. **Projected Growth 2012–22:** 11.3%. **Projected Annual Openings**: 5,590.

Typical Entry Requirements. Education: Doctoral degree (in Psychology). **Work Experience:** None. **On-the-Job Training:** Residency.

Related Majors: Psychology, p. 132.

JOB SPECIALIZATION: CLINICAL PSYCHOLOGISTS

Diagnose or evaluate mental and emotional disorders of individuals through observation, interview, and psychological tests, and formulate and administer programs of treatment.

Personality Type(s): Investigative–Social–Artistic. **Top Skills:** Science; Communication; Thought-Processing; Social. **Work Environment:** Indoors; sitting; disease or infections.

JOB SPECIALIZATION: COUNSELING PSYCHOLOGISTS

Assess and evaluate individuals' problems through the use of case history, interview, and observation and provide individual or group counseling services to assist individuals in achieving more effective personal, social, educational, and vocational development and adjustment.

Personality Type(s): Social–Investigative–Artistic. **Top Skills:** Science; Social; Communication; Management; Thought-Processing. **Work Environment:** Indoors; sitting.

JOB SPECIALIZATION: SCHOOL PSYCHOLOGISTS

Investigate processes of learning and teaching and develop psychological principles and techniques applicable to educational problems.

Personality Type(s): Investigative–Social. **Top Skills:** Social; Thought-Processing; Communication; Technology/Programming. **Work Environment:** Indoors; sitting.

COACHES AND SCOUTS

Instruct or coach groups or individuals in the fundamentals of sports. Demonstrate techniques and methods of participation. May evaluate athletes' strengths and weaknesses as possible recruits or to improve the athletes' technique to prepare them for competition. Those required to hold teaching degrees should be reported in the appropriate teaching category.

Annual Earnings. Average: $29,150. **Middle 50%:** $19,330–$46,190.

Employment Outlook. Workforce 2012: 243,900. **Projected Growth 2012–22:** 14.8%. **Projected Annual Openings**: 10,850.

Personality Type(s): Social–Realistic–Enterprising. **Top Skills:** Thought-Processing; Social; Management; Science; Technology/Programming; Communication. **Work Environment:** Outdoors; indoors; standing; noisy; very hot or cold.

Typical Entry Requirements. Education: Bachelor's degree. **Work Experience:** None. **On-the-Job Training:** None.

Related Majors: Physical Education, p. 93.

COMPENSATION AND BENEFITS MANAGERS

Plan, direct, or coordinate compensation and benefits activities of an organization.

Annual Earnings. Average: $101,490. **Middle 50%:** $74,850–$137,760.

Employment Outlook. Workforce 2012: 20,700. **Projected Growth 2012–22:** 3.1%. **Projected Annual Openings**: 610.

Personality Type(s): Enterprising–Conventional–Social. **Top Skills:** Management; Social; Thought-Processing; Communication; Mathematics. **Work Environment:** Indoors; sitting.

Typical Entry Requirements. Education: Bachelor's degree. **Work Experience:** 5 years or more. **On-the-Job Training:** None.

Related Majors: Human Resources Management, p. 77.

COMPENSATION, BENEFITS, AND JOB ANALYSIS SPECIALISTS

Conduct programs of compensation and benefits and job analysis for employer. May specialize in specific areas, such as position classification and pension programs.

Annual Earnings. Average: $59,820. **Middle 50%:** $46,670–$75,150.

Employment Outlook. Workforce 2012: 91,700. **Projected Growth 2012–22:** 5.8%. **Projected Annual Openings**: 2,200.

Personality Type(s): Conventional–Enterprising. **Top Skills:** Mathematics; Science; Thought-Processing; Technology/Programming; Social; Management; Communication. **Work Environment:** Indoors; sitting.

Typical Entry Requirements. Education: Bachelor's degree. **Work Experience:** None. **On-the-Job Training:** None.

Related Majors: Human Resources Management, p. 77.

COMPUTER AND INFORMATION RESEARCH SCIENTISTS

Conduct research into fundamental computer and information science as theorists, designers, or inventors. Develop solutions to problems in the field of computer hardware and software.

Annual Earnings. Average: $106,290. **Middle 50%:** $83,210–$129,750.

Employment Outlook. Workforce 2012: 26,700. **Projected Growth 2012–22:** 15.3%. **Projected Annual Openings:** 830.

Personality Type(s): Investigative–Realistic–Conventional. **Top Skills:** Technology/Programming; Management; Thought-Processing; Mathematics; Science; Equipment Use/Maintenance; Social; Communication. **Work Environment:** Indoors; sitting; using hands; repetitive motions.

Typical Entry Requirements. Education: Doctoral degree (in Computer Science or Computer Engineering). **Work Experience:** None. **On-the-Job Training:** None.

Related Majors: Computer Science, p. 85.

COMPUTER AND INFORMATION SYSTEMS MANAGERS

Plan, direct, or coordinate activities in such fields as electronic data processing, information systems, systems analysis, and computer programming.

Annual Earnings. Average: $123,950. **Middle 50%:** $96,850–$156,560.

Employment Outlook. Workforce 2012: 332,700. **Projected Growth 2012–22:** 15.3%. **Projected Annual Openings**: 9,710.

Personality Type(s): Enterprising–Conventional–Investigative. **Top Skills:** Equipment Use/Maintenance; Management; Technology/Programming; Mathematics; Thought-Processing; Science; Communication; Social. **Work Environment:** Indoors; sitting; using hands.

Typical Entry Requirements. Education: Bachelor's degree. **Work Experience:** 5 years or more. **On-the-Job Training:** None.

Related Majors: Computer Science, p. 85; Management Information Systems, p. 79.

COMPUTER HARDWARE ENGINEERS

Research, design, develop, or test computer or computer-related equipment for commercial, industrial, military, or scientific use. May supervise the manufacturing and installation of computer or computer-related equipment and components.

Annual Earnings. Average: $104,250. **Middle 50%:** $81,500–$130,060.

Employment Outlook. Workforce 2012: 83,300. **Projected Growth 2012–22:** 7.4%. **Projected Annual Openings**: 2,410.

Personality Type(s): Investigative–Realistic–Conventional. **Top Skills:** Science; Technology/Programming; Thought-Processing; Social; Management; Installation; Communication; Equipment Use/Maintenance; Mathematics. **Work Environment:** Indoors; sitting.

Typical Entry Requirements. Education: Bachelor's degree. **Work Experience:** None. **On-the-Job Training:** None.

Related Majors: Computer Engineering, p. 104.

COMPUTER NETWORK ARCHITECTS

Design and implement computer and information networks, such as local area networks (LAN), wide area networks (WAN), intranets, extranets, and other data communications networks. Perform network modeling, analysis, and planning. May also design network and computer security measures. May research and recommend network and data communications hardware and software.

Annual Earnings. Average: $95,380. **Middle 50%:** $72,070–$119,690.

Employment Outlook. Workforce 2012: 143,400. **Projected Growth 2012–22:** 14.6%. **Projected Annual Openings:** 4,350.

Personality Type(s): Investigative–Conventional–Enterprising. **Top Skills:** Technology/Programming; Science; Equipment Use/Maintenance; Installation; Thought-Processing; Communication; Management; Social; Mathematics. **Work Environment:** Indoors; sitting.

Typical Entry Requirements. Education: Bachelor's degree. **Work Experience:** 5 years or more. **On-the-Job Training:** None.

Related Majors: Computer Engineering, p. 104.

JOB SPECIALIZATION: TELECOMMUNICATIONS ENGINEERING SPECIALISTS

Design or configure voice, video, and data communications systems. Supervise installation and post-installation service and maintenance.

Personality Type(s): Realistic–Enterprising–Conventional. **Top Skills:** Technology/Programming; Installation; Thought-Processing; Social; Mathematics; Management; Equipment Use/Maintenance; Communication. **Work Environment:** Indoors; sitting.

COMPUTER NETWORK SUPPORT SPECIALISTS

Analyze, test, troubleshoot, and evaluate existing network systems, such as local area network (LAN), wide area network (WAN), and Internet systems or a segment of a network system. Perform network maintenance to ensure networks operate correctly with minimal interruption.

Annual Earnings. Average: $60,180. **Middle 50%:** $45,230–$78,360.

Employment Outlook. Workforce 2012: 174,600. **Projected Growth 2012–22:** 6.9%. **Projected Annual Openings**: 3,960.

Personality Type(s): Realistic–Enterprising–Conventional. **Top Skills:** Installation; Equipment Use/Maintenance; Technology/Programming; Communication; Thought-Processing; Mathematics. **Work Environment:** Indoors; sitting; using hands; repetitive motions.

Typical Entry Requirements. Education: Associate's degree. **Work Experience:** None. **On-the-Job Training:** None.

Related Majors: Computer Science, p. 85.

COMPUTER OCCUPATIONS, ALL OTHER

All computer occupations not listed separately.

Annual Earnings. Average: $82,340. **Middle 50%:** $62,890–$103,640.

Employment Outlook. Workforce 2012: 205,800. **Projected Growth 2012–22:** 3.8%. **Projected Annual Openings**: 4,020.

Typical Entry Requirements. Education: Bachelor's degree. **Work Experience:** None. **On-the-Job Training:** None.

Related Majors: Computer Science, p. 85.

JOB SPECIALIZATION: BUSINESS INTELLIGENCE ANALYSTS

Produce financial and market intelligence by querying data repositories and generating periodic reports. Devise methods for identifying data patterns and trends in available information sources.

Personality Type(s): Investigative–Enterprising–Conventional. **Top Skills:** Mathematics; Technology/Programming; Social; Communication; Management; Thought-Processing. **Work Environment:** Indoors; sitting.

JOB SPECIALIZATION: COMPUTER SYSTEMS ENGINEERS/ARCHITECTS

Design and develop solutions to complex applications problems, system administration issues, or network concerns. Perform systems management and integration functions.

Personality Type(s): Investigative–Realistic–Conventional. **Top Skills:** Science; Technology/Programming; Communication; Equipment Use/ Maintenance; Installation; Management; Mathematics; Social; Thought-Processing. **Work Environment:** Indoors; sitting; repetitive motions.

JOB SPECIALIZATION: DATA WAREHOUSING SPECIALISTS

Design, model, or implement corporate data warehousing activities. Program and configure warehouses of database information and provide support to warehouse users.

Personality Type(s): Investigative–Conventional. **Top Skills:** No data available. **Work Environment:** No data available.

JOB SPECIALIZATION: DATABASE ARCHITECTS

Design strategies for enterprise database systems and set standards for operations, programming, and security. Design and construct large relational databases. Integrate new systems with existing warehouse structure and refine system performance and functionality.

Personality Type(s): Investigative–Conventional–Enterprising. **Top Skills:** No data available. **Work Environment:** No data available.

JOB SPECIALIZATION: DOCUMENT MANAGEMENT SPECIALISTS

Implement and administer enterprise-wide document management systems and related procedures that allow organizations to capture, store, retrieve, share, and destroy electronic records and documents.

Personality Type(s): Conventional. **Top Skills:** Social; Technology/ Programming; Thought-Processing; Installation; Communication; Management. **Work Environment:** Indoors; sitting.

JOB SPECIALIZATION: GEOGRAPHIC INFORMATION SYSTEMS TECHNICIANS

Assist scientists, technologists, or related professionals in building, maintaining, modifying, or using geographic information systems (GIS) databases. May also perform some custom application development or provide user support.

Personality Type(s): Investigative–Realistic–Conventional. **Top Skills:** Technology/Programming; Mathematics; Science; Thought-Processing; Installation; Communication. **Work Environment:** Indoors; sitting; using hands; repetitive motions.

JOB SPECIALIZATION: GEOSPATIAL INFORMATION SCIENTISTS AND TECHNOLOGISTS

Research or develop geospatial technologies. May produce databases, perform applications programming, or coordinate projects. May specialize in areas such as agriculture, mining, health care, retail trade, urban planning, or military intelligence.

Personality Type(s): Investigative–Realistic–Conventional. **Top Skills:** Science; Social; Technology/Programming; Mathematics; Communication; Management; Thought-Processing. **Work Environment:** Indoors; sitting; using hands; repetitive motions.

JOB SPECIALIZATION: INFORMATION TECHNOLOGY PROJECT MANAGERS

Plan, initiate, and manage information technology (IT) projects. Lead and guide the work of technical staff. Serve as liaison between business and technical aspects of projects. Plan project stages and assess business implications for each stage. Monitor progress to assure deadlines, standards, and cost targets are met.

Personality Type(s): Enterprising–Conventional. **Top Skills:** Management; Thought-Processing; Technology/Programming; Social; Mathematics; Communication. **Work Environment:** Indoors; sitting.

JOB SPECIALIZATION: SEARCH MARKETING STRATEGISTS

Employ search marketing tactics to increase visibility and engagement with content, products, or services in Internet-enabled devices or interfaces. Examine search query behaviors on general or specialty search engines or other Internet-based content. Analyze research, data, or technology to understand user intent and measure outcomes for ongoing optimization.

Personality Type(s): Enterprising–Investigative–Conventional. **Top Skills:** Technology/Programming; Installation; Social; Thought-Processing; Communication; Management; Mathematics. **Work Environment:** Indoors; sitting; using hands.

JOB SPECIALIZATION: SOFTWARE QUALITY ASSURANCE ENGINEERS AND TESTERS

Develop and execute software test plans in order to identify software problems and their causes.

Personality Type(s): Investigative–Conventional–Realistic. **Top Skills:** Science; Installation; Technology/Programming; Communication; Equipment Use/Maintenance; Thought-Processing. **Work Environment:** Indoors; sitting; using hands; repetitive motions.

JOB SPECIALIZATION: VIDEO GAME DESIGNERS

Design core features of video games. Specify innovative game and role-play mechanics, story lines, and character biographies. Create and maintain design documentation. Guide and collaborate with production staff to produce games as designed.

Personality Type(s): Artistic–Enterprising. **Top Skills:** Technology/Programming; Management; Thought-Processing; Social; Mathematics; Communication. **Work Environment:** Indoors; sitting; using hands; repetitive motions.

JOB SPECIALIZATION: WEB ADMINISTRATORS

Manage web environment design, deployment, development and maintenance activities. Perform testing and quality assurance of websites and web applications.

Personality Type(s): Conventional–Enterprising–Investigative. **Top Skills:** Science; Technology/Programming; Communication; Social; Thought-Processing; Installation. **Work Environment:** Indoors; sitting; using hands; repetitive motions.

COMPUTER PROGRAMMERS

Create, modify, and test the code, forms, and script that allow computer applications to run. Work from specifications drawn up by software developers or other individuals. May assist software developers by analyzing user needs and designing software solutions. May develop and write computer programs to store, locate, and retrieve specific documents, data, and information.

Annual Earnings. Average: $76,140. **Middle 50%:** $57,940–$97,760.

Employment Outlook. Workforce 2012: 343,700. **Projected Growth 2012–22:** 8.3%. **Projected Annual Openings**: 11,810.

Personality Type(s): Investigative–Conventional. **Top Skills:** Technology/Programming; Science; Mathematics; Thought-Processing; Communication. **Work Environment:** Indoors; sitting; using hands; repetitive motions.

Typical Entry Requirements. Education: Bachelor's degree. **Work Experience:** None. **On-the-Job Training:** None.

Related Majors: Computer Science, p. 85; Management Information Systems, p. 79.

CONSTRUCTION MANAGERS

Plan, direct, or coordinate, usually through subordinate supervisory personnel, activities concerned with the construction and maintenance of structures, facilities, and systems. Participate in the conceptual development of a construction project and oversee its organization, scheduling, budgeting, and implementation. Includes managers in specialized construction fields, such as carpentry or plumbing.

Annual Earnings. Average: $84,410. **Middle 50%:** $64,890–$111,710.

Employment Outlook. Workforce 2012: 485,000. **Projected Growth 2012–22:** 16.1%. **Projected Annual Openings**: 15,460.

Personality Type(s): Enterprising–Realistic–Conventional. **Top Skills:** Mathematics; Management; Thought-Processing; Technology/ Programming; Communication; Science; Social. **Work Environment:** Indoors; outdoors; sitting; noisy.

Typical Entry Requirements. Education: Bachelor's degree. **Work Experience:** None. **On-the-Job Training:** Moderate-term on-the-job training.

Related Majors: Architecture, p. 67; Business Management and Administration, p. 74; Civil Engineering, p. 103.

CORRECTIONAL OFFICERS AND JAILERS

Guard inmates in penal or rehabilitative institutions in accordance with established regulations and procedures. May guard prisoners in transit between jail, courtroom, prison, or other point. Includes deputy sheriffs and police who spend the majority of their time guarding prisoners in correctional institutions.

Annual Earnings. Average: $39,550. **Middle 50%:** $31,620–$55,380.

Employment Outlook. Workforce 2012: 452,800. **Projected Growth 2012–22:** 4.9%. **Projected Annual Openings:** 14,240.

Personality Type(s): Realistic–Enterprising–Conventional. **Top Skills:** Social. **Work Environment:** Indoors; sitting; standing; walking and running; using hands; repetitive motions; noisy; very bright or dim lighting; contaminants; disease or infections.

Typical Entry Requirements. Education: High school diploma or equivalent. **Work Experience:** None. **On-the-Job Training:** Moderate-term on-the-job training.

Related Majors: Criminal Justice, p. 86.

COST ESTIMATORS

Prepare cost estimates for product manufacturing, construction projects, or services to aid management in bidding on or determining price of product or service. May specialize according to particular service performed or type of product manufactured.

Annual Earnings. Average: $59,460. **Middle 50%:** $44,710–$78,250.

Employment Outlook. Workforce 2012: 202,200. **Projected Growth 2012–22:** 26.2%. **Projected Annual Openings:** 11,800.

Personality Type(s): Conventional–Enterprising. **Top Skills:** Mathematics; Management; Communication; Social; Technology/ Programming; Thought-Processing. **Work Environment:** Indoors; sitting.

Typical Entry Requirements. Education: Bachelor's degree. **Work Experience:** None. **On-the-Job Training:** None.

Related Majors: Business Management and Administration, p. 74; Mechanical Engineering, p. 107.

CRAFT ARTISTS

Create or reproduce handmade objects for sale and exhibition using a variety of techniques, such as welding, weaving, pottery, and needlecraft.

Annual Earnings. Average: $30,400. **Middle 50%:** $22,400–$45,640.

Employment Outlook. Workforce 2012: 11,200. **Projected Growth 2012–22:** 3.3%. **Projected Annual Openings:** 300.

Personality Type(s): Artistic–Realistic–Enterprising. **Top Skills:** Technology/Programming; Equipment Use/Maintenance. **Work Environment:** Indoors; standing; using hands; repetitive motions; contaminants.

Typical Entry Requirements. Education: High school diploma or equivalent. **Work Experience:** None. **On-the-Job Training:** Long-term on-the-job training.

Related Majors: Studio Art, p. 140.

COUNSELORS, ALL OTHER

All counselors not listed separately.

Annual Earnings. Average: $43,620. **Middle 50%:** $32,570–$57,480.

Employment Outlook. Workforce 2012: 29,800. **Projected Growth 2012–22:** 19.4%. **Projected Annual Openings**: 1,210.

Personality Type(s): No data available. **Top Skills:** No data available. **Work Environment:** No data available.

Typical Entry Requirements. Education: Master's degree (in a counseling field). **Work Experience:** None. **On-the-Job Training:** None.

Related Majors: Social Work, p. 136.

CREDIT ANALYSTS

Analyze credit data and financial statements of individuals or firms to determine the degree of risk involved in extending credit or lending money. Prepare reports with credit information for use in decision making.

Annual Earnings. Average: $64,030. **Middle 50%:** $47,990–$87,520.

Employment Outlook. Workforce 2012: 61,800. **Projected Growth 2012–22:** 10.4%. **Projected Annual Openings**: 2,180.

Personality Type(s): Conventional–Enterprising. **Top Skills:** Mathematics; Thought-Processing; Communication. **Work Environment:** Indoors; sitting; repetitive motions.

Typical Entry Requirements. Education: Bachelor's degree. **Work Experience:** None. **On-the-Job Training:** None.

Related Majors: Accounting, p. 73; Finance, p. 75.

CURATORS

Administer collections, such as artwork, collectibles, historic items, or scientific specimens of museums or other institutions. May conduct instructional, research, or public service activities of institution.

Annual Earnings. Average: $50,550. **Middle 50%:** $37,270–$69,030.

Employment Outlook. Workforce 2012: 11,400. **Projected Growth 2012–22:** 12.5%. **Projected Annual Openings**: 390.

Personality Type(s): Enterprising–Conventional. **Top Skills:** Management; Thought-Processing; Technology/Programming; Social; Installation; Communication; Mathematics. **Work Environment:** Indoors; sitting.

Typical Entry Requirements. Education: Master's degree (in Art History, Archaeology, History, or Museum Studies). **Work Experience:** None. **On-the-Job Training:** None.

Related Majors: Art History, p. 69.

DANCERS

Perform dances. May perform on stage, for on-air broadcasting, or for video recording.

Annual Earnings. Average: No data available. **Middle 50%:** No data available.

Employment Outlook. Workforce 2012: 15,600. **Projected Growth 2012–22:** 5.9%. **Projected Annual Openings:** 540.

Personality Type(s): Artistic–Realistic. **Top Skills:** Social. **Work Environment:** Indoors; standing; walking and running; kneeling, crouching, stooping, or crawling; balancing; using hands; bending or twisting body; repetitive motions; very bright or dim lighting; contaminants.

Typical Entry Requirements. Education: High school diploma or equivalent. **Work Experience:** None. **On-the-Job Training:** Long-term on-the-job training.

Related Majors: Dance, p. 87.

DENTISTS, ALL OTHER SPECIALISTS

All dentists not listed separately.

Annual Earnings. Average: $163,450. **Middle 50%:** $114,450–$187,200+.

Employment Outlook. Workforce 2012: 6,400. **Projected Growth 2012–22:** 6.3%. **Projected Annual Openings**: 200.

Typical Entry Requirements. Education: Professional degree (in Dentistry). **Work Experience:** None. **On-the-Job Training:** Residency.

Related Majors: Pre-Professional Health (or any major, plus courses required for entry to dentistry school), p. 131.

DENTISTS, GENERAL

Examine, diagnose, and treat diseases, injuries, and malformations of teeth and gums. May treat diseases of nerve, pulp, and other dental tissues affecting oral hygiene and retention of teeth. May fit dental appliances or provide preventive care.

Annual Earnings. Average: $146,340. **Middle 50%:** $105,520–$187,200+.

Employment Outlook. Workforce 2012: 125,800. **Projected Growth 2012–22:** 16.3%. **Projected Annual Openings**: 5,120.

Personality Type(s): Investigative–Realistic–Social. **Top Skills:** Science; Technology/Programming; Management; Social; Equipment Use/Maintenance; Thought-Processing; Communication; Mathematics. **Work Environment:** Indoors; sitting; using hands; bending or twisting body; repetitive motions; noisy; contaminants; cramped work space, awkward positions; radiation; disease or infections.

Typical Entry Requirements. Education: Professional degree (in Dentistry). **Work Experience:** None. **On-the-Job Training:** None.

Related Majors: Pre-Professional Health (or any major, plus courses required for entry to dentistry school), p. 131.

DIRECTORS, RELIGIOUS ACTIVITIES AND EDUCATION

Plan, direct, or coordinate programs designed to promote the religious education or activities of a denominational group. May provide counseling and guidance relative to marital, health, financial, and religious problems.

Annual Earnings. Average: $38,160. **Middle 50%:** $25,720–$56,980.

Employment Outlook. Workforce 2012: 134,200. **Projected Growth 2012–22:** 8.4%. **Projected Annual Openings**: 5,700.

Personality Type(s): Enterprising–Social–Conventional. **Top Skills:** Management; Social; Thought-Processing; Mathematics; Communication. **Work Environment:** Indoors; standing.

Typical Entry Requirements. Education: Bachelor's degree. **Work Experience:** Less than 5 years. **On-the-Job Training:** None.

Related Majors: Religious Studies, p. 135.

ECONOMISTS

Conduct research, prepare reports, or formulate plans to address economic problems related to the production and distribution of goods and services or monetary and fiscal policy. May collect and process economic and statistical data using sampling techniques and econometric methods.

Annual Earnings. Average: $93,070. **Middle 50%:** $67,380–$126,230.

Employment Outlook. Workforce 2012: 16,900. **Projected Growth 2012–22:** 13.9%. **Projected Annual Openings**: 740.

Personality Type(s): Investigative–Conventional–Enterprising. **Top Skills:** Mathematics; Science; Communication; Thought-Processing; Social. **Work Environment:** Indoors; sitting.

Typical Entry Requirements. Education: Master's degree (in Economics). **Work Experience:** None. **On-the-Job Training:** None.

Related Majors: Economics (or another major with emphasis on mathematics), p. 88.

JOB SPECIALIZATION: ENVIRONMENTAL ECONOMISTS

Conduct economic analysis related to environmental protection and use of the natural environment, such as water, air, land, and renewable energy resources. Evaluate and quantify benefits, costs, incentives, and impacts of alternative options using economic principles and statistical techniques.

Personality Type(s): Investigative–Enterprising–Conventional. **Top Skills:** Mathematics; Communication; Thought-Processing; Technology/ Programming; Science; Management; Social. **Work Environment:** Indoors; sitting.

EDITORS

Plan, coordinate, or edit content of material for publication. May review proposals and drafts for possible publication. Includes technical editors.

Annual Earnings. Average: $54,150. **Middle 50%:** $39,190–$75,030.

Employment Outlook. Workforce 2012: 115,300. **Projected Growth 2012–22:** -2.4%. **Projected Annual Openings**: 2,800.

Personality Type(s): Artistic–Enterprising–Conventional. **Top Skills:** Communication; Social; Thought-Processing; Management; Mathematics. **Work Environment:** Indoors; sitting; using hands; repetitive motions; noisy.

Typical Entry Requirements. Education: Bachelor's degree. **Work Experience:** Less than 5 years. **On-the-Job Training:** None.

Related Majors: Communication, p. 84; English, p. 111; Journalism, p. 119.

ELECTRICAL ENGINEERS

Research, design, develop, test, or supervise the manufacturing and installation of electrical equipment, components, or systems for commercial, industrial, military, or scientific use.

Annual Earnings. Average: $89,180. **Middle 50%:** $70,650–$112,560.

Employment Outlook. Workforce 2012: 166,100. **Projected Growth 2012–22:** 4.7%. **Projected Annual Openings**: 4,410.

Personality Type(s): Investigative–Realistic. **Top Skills:** Mathematics; Science; Management; Equipment Use/Maintenance; Technology/Programming; Thought-Processing; Communication; Social. **Work Environment:** Indoors; sitting; noisy.

Typical Entry Requirements. Education: Bachelor's degree. **Work Experience:** None. **On-the-Job Training:** None.

Related Majors: Electrical Engineering, p. 105.

ELECTRONICS ENGINEERS, EXCEPT COMPUTER

Research, design, develop, or test electronic components and systems for commercial, industrial, military, or scientific use employing knowledge of electronic theory and materials properties. Design electronic circuits and components for use in fields such as telecommunications, aerospace guidance and propulsion control, acoustics, or instruments and controls.

Annual Earnings. Average: $94,250. **Middle 50%:** $74,590–$117,040.

Employment Outlook. Workforce 2012: 140,000. **Projected Growth 2012–22:** 3.4%. **Projected Annual Openings**: 3,530.

Personality Type(s): Investigative–Realistic. **Top Skills:** Technology/Programming; Equipment Use/Maintenance; Science; Mathematics; Thought-Processing; Social; Management; Communication; Installation. **Work Environment:** Indoors; sitting; using hands; noisy.

Typical Entry Requirements. Education: Bachelor's degree. **Work Experience:** None. **On-the-Job Training:** None.

Related Majors: Electrical Engineering, p. 105.

JOB SPECIALIZATION: RADIO FREQUENCY IDENTIFICATION DEVICE SPECIALISTS

Design and implement radio frequency identification device (RFID) systems used to track shipments or goods.

Personality Type(s): Realistic–Investigative–Conventional. **Top Skills:** No data available. **Work Environment:** No data available.

ELEMENTARY SCHOOL TEACHERS, EXCEPT SPECIAL EDUCATION

Teach students basic academic, social, and other formative skills in public or private schools at the elementary level.

Annual Earnings. Average: $53,590. **Middle 50%:** $43,070–$67,730.

Employment Outlook. Workforce 2012: 1,361,200. **Projected Growth 2012–22:** 12.3%. **Projected Annual Openings:** 46,740.

Personality Type(s): Social–Artistic–Conventional. **Top Skills:** Mathematics; Thought-Processing; Technology/Programming; Science; Communication; Social. **Work Environment:** Indoors; standing; noisy.

Typical Entry Requirements. Education: Bachelor's degree. **Work Experience:** None. **On-the-Job Training:** Student teaching.

Related Majors: Elementary Education (or a subject to be taught; see your state's requirements), p. 91.

ENTERTAINERS AND PERFORMERS, SPORTS AND RELATED WORKERS, ALL OTHER

All entertainers and performers, sports and related workers not listed separately.

Annual Earnings. Average: No data available. **Middle 50%:** No data available.

Employment Outlook. Workforce 2012: 36,600. **Projected Growth 2012–22:** 7.3%. **Projected Annual Openings**: 720.

Typical Entry Requirements. Education: High school diploma or equivalent. **Work Experience:** None. **On-the-Job Training:** None.

Related Majors: Theater Arts, p. 141.

ENVIRONMENTAL SCIENTISTS AND SPECIALISTS, INCLUDING HEALTH

Conduct research or perform investigation for the purpose of identifying, abating, or eliminating sources of pollutants or hazards that affect either the environment or the health of the population. Using knowledge of various scientific disciplines, may collect, synthesize, study, report, and recommend action based on data derived from measurements or observations of air, food, soil, water, and other sources.

Annual Earnings. Average: $65,090. **Middle 50%:** $48,780–$86,880.

Employment Outlook. Workforce 2012: 90,000. **Projected Growth 2012–22:** 14.6%. **Projected Annual Openings**: 3,970.

Personality Type(s): Investigative–Realistic–Conventional. **Top Skills:** Science; Mathematics; Communication; Social; Technology/ Programming; Thought-Processing; Management. **Work Environment:** Indoors; sitting.

Typical Entry Requirements. Education: Bachelor's degree. **Work Experience:** None. **On-the-Job Training:** None.

Related Majors: Environmental Science, p. 111.

JOB SPECIALIZATION: CLIMATE CHANGE ANALYSTS

Research and analyze policy developments related to climate change. Make climate-related recommendations for actions such as legislation, awareness campaigns, or fundraising approaches.

Personality Type(s): Investigative–Enterprising. **Top Skills:** Management; Technology/Programming; Social; Thought-Processing; Science; Mathematics; Communication. **Work Environment:** Indoors; sitting.

JOB SPECIALIZATION: ENVIRONMENTAL RESTORATION PLANNERS

Collaborate with field and biology staff to oversee the implementation of restoration projects and to develop new products. Process and synthesize complex scientific data into practical strategies for restoration, monitoring, or management.

Personality Type(s): Investigative–Realistic–Enterprising. **Top Skills:** Science; Thought-Processing; Communication; Installation; Management; Mathematics; Social; Technology/Programming. **Work Environment:** Indoors; outdoors; sitting.

JOB SPECIALIZATION: INDUSTRIAL ECOLOGISTS

Apply principles and processes of natural ecosystems to develop models for efficient industrial systems. Use knowledge from the physical and social sciences to maximize effective use of natural resources in the production and use of goods and services. Examine societal issues and their relationship with both technical systems and the environment.

Personality Type(s): Investigative–Enterprising. **Top Skills:** No data available. **Work Environment:** No data available.

FAMILY AND GENERAL PRACTITIONERS

Physicians who diagnose, treat, and help prevent diseases and injuries that commonly occur in the general population. May refer patients to specialists when needed for further diagnosis or treatment.

Annual Earnings. Average: $176,530. **Middle 50%:** $130,780–$187,200+.

Employment Outlook. Workforce 2012: 124,000. **Projected Growth 2012–22:** 14.6%. **Projected Annual Openings:** 4,920.

Personality Type(s): Investigative–Social. **Top Skills:** Science; Communication; Thought-Processing; Mathematics; Management; Social. **Work Environment:** Indoors; sitting; disease or infections.

Typical Entry Requirements. Education: Professional degree (in Medicine). **Work Experience:** None. **On-the-Job Training:** Internship/residency.

Related Majors: Pre-Professional Health (or any major, plus courses required for entry to medical school), p. 131.

FARMERS, RANCHERS, AND OTHER AGRICULTURAL MANAGERS

Plan, direct, or coordinate the management or operation of farms, ranches, greenhouses, aquacultural operations, nurseries, timber tracts, or other agricultural establishments. May hire, train, and supervise farm workers or contract for services to carry out the day-to-day activities of the managed operation. May engage in or supervise planting, cultivating, harvesting, and financial and marketing activities.

Annual Earnings. Average: $70,110. **Middle 50%:** $48,080–$91,290.

Employment Outlook. Workforce 2012: 930,600. **Projected Growth 2012–22:** -19.3%. **Projected Annual Openings:** 15,020.

Typical Entry Requirements. Education: High school diploma or equivalent. **Work Experience:** 5 years or more. **On-the-Job Training:** None.

Related Majors: Agricultural Business, p. 65; Agronomy, p. 66.

JOB SPECIALIZATION: AQUACULTURAL MANAGERS

Direct and coordinate, through subordinate supervisory personnel, activities of workers engaged in fish hatchery production for corporations, cooperatives, or other owners.

Personality Type(s): Enterprising–Realistic–Conventional. **Top Skills:** Equipment Use/Maintenance; Science; Technology/Programming; Thought-Processing; Social; Management; Communication. **Work Environment:** Outdoors; indoors; standing; using hands; noisy; very hot or cold; contaminants.

JOB SPECIALIZATION: FARM AND RANCH MANAGERS

Plan, direct, or coordinate the management or operation of farms, ranches, greenhouses, aquacultural operations, nurseries, timber tracts, or other agricultural establishments. May hire, train, or supervise farm workers or contract for services to carry out the day-to-day activities of the managed operation. May engage in or supervise planting, cultivating, harvesting, financial, or marketing activities.

Personality Type(s): Enterprising–Realistic–Conventional. **Top Skills:** Equipment Use/Maintenance; Management; Mathematics; Science; Thought-Processing; Communication; Social; Technology/Programming. **Work Environment:** Outdoors; indoors; using hands; noisy; very hot or cold; contaminants; hazardous equipment; minor burns, cuts, bites, or stings.

JOB SPECIALIZATION: NURSERY AND GREENHOUSE MANAGERS

Plan, organize, direct, control, and coordinate activities of workers engaged in propagating, cultivating, and harvesting horticultural specialties, such as trees, shrubs, flowers, mushrooms, and other plants.

Personality Type(s): Enterprising–Realistic–Conventional. **Top Skills:** Management; Science; Thought-Processing; Communication; Equipment Use/Maintenance; Social. **Work Environment:** Outdoors; indoors; standing; walking and running; kneeling, crouching, stooping, or crawling; noisy; very hot or cold; contaminants; hazardous conditions; minor burns, cuts, bites, or stings.

FINANCIAL ANALYSTS

Conduct quantitative analyses of information affecting investment programs of public or private institutions.

Annual Earnings. Average: $78,380. **Middle 50%:** $60,010–$106,470.

Employment Outlook. Workforce 2012: 253,000. **Projected Growth 2012–22:** 15.5%. **Projected Annual Openings:** 10,090.

Personality Type(s): Conventional–Investigative–Enterprising. **Top Skills:** Management; Thought-Processing; Social; Mathematics; Communication. **Work Environment:** Indoors; sitting.

Typical Entry Requirements. Education: Bachelor's degree. **Work Experience:** None. **On-the-Job Training:** None.

Related Majors: Finance, p. 75.

FINANCIAL EXAMINERS

Enforce or ensure compliance with laws and regulations governing financial and securities institutions and financial and real estate transactions. May examine, verify, or authenticate records.

Annual Earnings. Average: $76,890. **Middle 50%:** $57,440–$109,300.

Employment Outlook. Workforce 2012: 29,200. **Projected Growth 2012–22:** 6.3%. **Projected Annual Openings**: 920.

Personality Type(s): Enterprising–Conventional. **Top Skills:** Management; Social; Thought-Processing; Communication; Mathematics. **Work Environment:** Indoors; sitting.

Typical Entry Requirements. Education: Bachelor's degree. **Work Experience:** None. **On-the-Job Training:** Moderate-term on-the-job training.

Related Majors: Accounting, p. 73.

FINANCIAL MANAGERS

Plan, direct, or coordinate accounting, investing, banking, insurance, securities, and other financial activities of a branch, office, or department of an establishment.

Annual Earnings. Average: $112,700. **Middle 50%:** $81,780–$153,970.

Employment Outlook. Workforce 2012: 532,100. **Projected Growth 2012–22:** 8.9%. **Projected Annual Openings**: 14,690.

Typical Entry Requirements. Education: Bachelor's degree. **Work Experience:** 5 years or more. **On-the-Job Training:** None.

Related Majors: Finance, p. 75.

JOB SPECIALIZATION: FINANCIAL MANAGERS, BRANCH OR DEPARTMENT

Direct and coordinate financial activities of workers in a branch, office, or department of an establishment, such as branch bank, brokerage firm, risk and insurance department, or credit department.

Personality Type(s): Enterprising–Conventional. **Top Skills:** Management; Social; Communication; Thought-Processing; Mathematics. **Work Environment:** Indoors; sitting.

JOB SPECIALIZATION: TREASURERS AND CONTROLLERS

Direct financial activities, such as planning, procurement, and investments for all or part of an organization.

Personality Type(s): Conventional–Enterprising. **Top Skills:** Thought-Processing; Management; Mathematics; Social; Communication. **Work Environment:** Indoors; sitting.

FINANCIAL SPECIALISTS, ALL OTHER

All financial specialists not listed separately.

Annual Earnings. Average: $62,510. **Middle 50%:** $45,750–$83,230.

Employment Outlook. Workforce 2012: 155,800. **Projected Growth 2012–22:** 6.1%. **Projected Annual Openings**: 2,580.

Typical Entry Requirements. Education: Bachelor's degree. **Work Experience:** None. **On-the-Job Training:** Moderate-term on-the-job training.

Related Majors: Finance, p. 75.

JOB SPECIALIZATION: FINANCIAL QUANTITATIVE ANALYSTS

Develop quantitative financial products used to inform individuals or financial institutions engaged in saving, lending, investing, borrowing, or managing risk. Investigate methods for financial analysis to create mathematical models used to develop improved analytical tools or advanced financial investment instruments.

Personality Type(s): Investigative–Conventional. **Top Skills:** No data available. **Work Environment:** No data available.

JOB SPECIALIZATION: FRAUD EXAMINERS, INVESTIGATORS, AND ANALYSTS

Obtain evidence, take statements, produce reports, and testify to findings regarding resolution of fraud allegations. May coordinate fraud detection and prevention activities.

Personality Type(s): Enterprising–Investigative–Conventional. **Top Skills:** Management; Social; Thought-Processing; Mathematics; Communication. **Work Environment:** Indoors; sitting.

JOB SPECIALIZATION: INVESTMENT UNDERWRITERS

Manage communications or negotiations between corporate issuers of securities and clients regarding private equity investments. Underwrite the issuance of securities to provide capital for client growth. Negotiate and structure the terms of mergers or acquisitions.

Personality Type(s): Conventional–Enterprising. **Top Skills:** No data available. **Work Environment:** No data available.

JOB SPECIALIZATION: RISK MANAGEMENT SPECIALISTS

Analyze and manage risk management issues by identifying, measuring, and making decisions on operational or enterprise risks for an organization.

Personality Type(s): Conventional–Enterprising–Investigative. **Top Skills:** Mathematics; Communication; Thought-Processing; Technology/Programming; Social; Management. **Work Environment:** Indoors; sitting.

FINE ARTISTS, INCLUDING PAINTERS, SCULPTORS, AND ILLUSTRATORS

Create original artwork using any of a wide variety of media and techniques.

Annual Earnings. Average: $42,610. **Middle 50%:** $27,160–$62,350.

Employment Outlook. Workforce 2012: 28,800. **Projected Growth 2012–22:** 3.8%. **Projected Annual Openings**: 790.

Personality Type(s): Artistic–Realistic. **Top Skills:** Technology/ Programming; Installation; Management. **Work Environment:** Indoors; standing; using hands; repetitive motions; contaminants.

Typical Entry Requirements. Education: High school diploma or equivalent. **Work Experience:** None. **On-the-Job Training:** Long-term on-the-job training.

Related Majors: Studio Art, p. 140.

FIRST-LINE SUPERVISORS OF CORRECTIONAL OFFICERS

Directly supervise and coordinate activities of correctional officers and jailers.

Annual Earnings. Average: $57,700. **Middle 50%:** $43,830–$77,170.

Employment Outlook. Workforce 2012: 46,700. **Projected Growth 2012–22:** 4.0%. **Projected Annual Openings**: 1,800.

Personality Type(s): Enterprising–Conventional–Realistic. **Top Skills:** Social; Communication; Thought-Processing; Management. **Work Environment:** Indoors; outdoors; standing; noisy; contaminants; disease or infections.

Typical Entry Requirements. Education: High school diploma or equivalent. **Work Experience:** Less than 5 years. **On-the-Job Training:** Moderate-term on-the-job training.

Related Majors: Criminal Justice, p. 86.

FIRST-LINE SUPERVISORS OF FARMING, FISHING, AND FORESTRY WORKERS

Directly supervise and coordinate the activities of agricultural, forestry, aquacultural, and related workers.

Annual Earnings. Average: $43,480. **Middle 50%:** $32,180–$56,830.

Employment Outlook. Workforce 2012: 45,900. **Projected Growth 2012–22:** -2.5%. **Projected Annual Openings**: 970.

Typical Entry Requirements. Education: High school diploma or equivalent. **Work Experience:** Less than 5 years. **On-the-Job Training:** None.

Related Majors: Agronomy, p. 66.

JOB SPECIALIZATION: FIRST-LINE SUPERVISORS OF AGRICULTURAL CROP AND HORTICULTURAL WORKERS

Directly supervise and coordinate activities of agricultural crop or horticultural workers.

Personality Type(s): Realistic–Enterprising–Conventional. **Top Skills:** Management; Equipment Use/Maintenance; Mathematics; Science; Social; Thought-Processing. **Work Environment:** Outdoors; indoors; walking and running; noisy; very hot or cold; contaminants; hazardous equipment; minor burns, cuts, bites, or stings.

JOB SPECIALIZATION: FIRST-LINE SUPERVISORS OF ANIMAL HUSBANDRY AND ANIMAL CARE WORKERS

Directly supervise and coordinate activities of animal husbandry or animal care workers.

Personality Type(s): Enterprising–Realistic. **Top Skills:** Equipment Use/Maintenance; Management; Science; Social; Technology/Programming; Communication; Thought-Processing; Mathematics. **Work Environment:**

Outdoors; standing; walking and running; using hands; noisy; very hot or cold; contaminants; hazardous conditions; hazardous equipment; minor burns, cuts, bites, or stings.

JOB SPECIALIZATION: FIRST-LINE SUPERVISORS OF AQUACULTURAL WORKERS

Directly supervise and coordinate activities of aquacultural workers.

Personality Type(s): Enterprising–Realistic–Conventional. **Top Skills:** Management; Science; Thought-Processing; Communication; Equipment Use/Maintenance; Mathematics; Social; Technology/Programming. **Work Environment:** Outdoors; indoors; standing; noisy; very hot or cold; very bright or dim lighting; contaminants; hazardous equipment; minor burns, cuts, bites, or stings.

JOB SPECIALIZATION: FIRST-LINE SUPERVISORS OF LOGGING WORKERS

Directly supervise and coordinate activities of logging workers.

Personality Type(s): Enterprising–Realistic–Conventional. **Top Skills:** Equipment Use/Maintenance; Management; Social; Technology/Programming; Thought-Processing; Mathematics; Communication. **Work Environment:** Outdoors; sitting; using hands; repetitive motions; noisy; very hot or cold; contaminants; hazardous equipment; minor burns, cuts, bites, or stings.

FIRST-LINE SUPERVISORS OF POLICE AND DETECTIVES

Directly supervise and coordinate activities of members of police force.

Annual Earnings. Average: $79,190. **Middle 50%:** $60,500–$102,600.

Employment Outlook. Workforce 2012: 103,700. **Projected Growth 2012–22:** 4.9%. **Projected Annual Openings:** 3,570.

Personality Type(s): Enterprising–Social–Conventional. **Top Skills:** Management; Social; Communication; Thought-Processing; Mathematics; Science. **Work Environment:** Indoors; outdoors; sitting; noisy; very hot or cold; very bright or dim lighting; contaminants; hazardous equipment.

Typical Entry Requirements. Education: High school diploma or equivalent. **Work Experience:** Less than 5 years. **On-the-Job Training:** Moderate-term on-the-job training.

Related Majors: Criminal Justice, p. 86.

FITNESS TRAINERS AND AEROBICS INSTRUCTORS

Instruct or coach groups or individuals in exercise activities. Demonstrate techniques and form, observe participants, and explain to them corrective measures necessary to improve their skills.

Annual Earnings. Average: $33,020. **Middle 50%:** $21,110–$48,590.

Employment Outlook. Workforce 2012: 267,000. **Projected Growth 2012–22:** 12.5%. **Projected Annual Openings**: 6,500.

Personality Type(s): Social–Realistic–Enterprising. **Top Skills:** Technology/Programming; Social. **Work Environment:** Indoors; standing; walking and running; bending or twisting body; repetitive motions.

Typical Entry Requirements. Education: High school diploma or equivalent. **Work Experience:** None. **On-the-Job Training:** Short-term on-the-job training.

Related Majors: Physical Education, p. 93.

FOOD SERVICE MANAGERS

Plan, direct, or coordinate activities of an organization or department that serves food and beverages.

Annual Earnings. Average: $48,080. **Middle 50%:** $38,480–$62,890.

Employment Outlook. Workforce 2012: 321,400. **Projected Growth 2012–22:** 1.6%. **Projected Annual Openings**: 6,240.

Personality Type(s): Enterprising–Conventional–Realistic. **Top Skills:** Management; Equipment Use/Maintenance; Social; Thought-Processing; Mathematics; Science. **Work Environment:** Indoors; standing; walking and running; using hands; repetitive motions; noisy; contaminants; minor burns, cuts, bites, or stings.

Typical Entry Requirements. Education: High school diploma or equivalent. **Work Experience:** Less than 5 years. **On-the-Job Training:** None.

Related Majors: Hospitality Management, p. 76.

GENERAL AND OPERATIONS MANAGERS

Plan, direct, or coordinate the operations of public or private sector organizations. Duties and responsibilities include formulating policies, managing daily operations, and planning the use of materials and human resources, but are too diverse and general in nature to be classified in any one functional area of management or administration, such as personnel, purchasing, or administrative services.

Annual Earnings. Average: $96,430. **Middle 50%:** $66,190–$147,350.

Employment Outlook. Workforce 2012: 1,972,700. **Projected Growth 2012–22:** 12.4%. **Projected Annual Openings**: 61,310.

Personality Type(s): Enterprising–Conventional–Social. **Top Skills:** Management; Thought-Processing; Communication; Social. **Work Environment:** Indoors; sitting; standing; noisy.

Typical Entry Requirements. Education: Bachelor's degree. **Work Experience:** Less than 5 years. **On-the-Job Training:** None.

Related Majors: Business Management and Administration, p. 74; Finance, p. 75.

GEOSCIENTISTS, EXCEPT HYDROLOGISTS AND GEOGRAPHERS

Study the composition, structure, and other physical aspects of the Earth. May use geological, physics, and mathematics knowledge in exploration for oil, gas, minerals, or underground water; or in waste disposal, land reclamation, or other environmental problems. May study the Earth's internal composition, atmospheres, oceans, and its magnetic, electrical, and gravitational forces. Includes mineralogists, crystallographers, paleontologists, stratigraphers, geodesists, and seismologists.

Annual Earnings. Average: $91,920. **Middle 50%:** $63,620–$134,390.

Employment Outlook. Workforce 2012: 38,200. **Projected Growth 2012–22:** 15.8%. **Projected Annual Openings**: 1,730.

Personality Type(s): Investigative–Realistic. **Top Skills:** Science; Mathematics; Communication; Social; Thought-Processing. **Work Environment:** Indoors; outdoors; sitting.

Typical Entry Requirements. Education: Bachelor's degree. **Work Experience:** None. **On-the-Job Training:** None.

Related Majors: Geology (or another science with course work in geology), p. 113.

GRAPHIC DESIGNERS

Design or create graphics to meet specific commercial or promotional needs, such as packaging, displays, or logos. May use a variety of mediums to achieve artistic or decorative effects.

Annual Earnings. Average: $44,830. **Middle 50%:** $34,040–$60,510.

Employment Outlook. Workforce 2012: 259,500. **Projected Growth 2012–22:** 6.7%. **Projected Annual Openings**: 8,600.

Personality Type(s): Artistic–Realistic–Enterprising. **Top Skills:** Technology/Programming; Thought-Processing. **Work Environment:** Indoors; sitting; using hands; repetitive motions.

Typical Entry Requirements. Education: Bachelor's degree. **Work Experience:** None. **On-the-Job Training:** None.

Related Majors: Graphic Design, p. 114.

HEALTH-CARE SOCIAL WORKERS

Provide individuals, families, and groups with the psychosocial support needed to cope with chronic, acute, or terminal illnesses. Services include advising family care givers, providing patient education and counseling, and making referrals for other services. May also provide care and case management or interventions designed to promote health, prevent disease, and address barriers to access to health care.

Annual Earnings. Average: $50,820. **Middle 50%:** $39,840–$62,860.

Employment Outlook. Workforce 2012: 146,200. **Projected Growth 2012–22:** 26.8%. **Projected Annual Openings:** 7,020.

Personality Type(s): Social–Investigative. **Top Skills:** Science; Social; Management; Thought-Processing; Communication. **Work Environment:** Indoors; sitting; disease or infections.

Typical Entry Requirements. Education: Master's degree (in Social Work). **Work Experience:** None. **On-the-Job Training:** Internship.

Related Majors: Social Work (or any major, plus courses required for entry to master's program in social work), p. 136.

HISTORIANS

Research, analyze, record, and interpret the past as recorded in sources, such as government and institutional records, newspapers and other periodicals, photographs, interviews, films, electronic media, and unpublished manuscripts, such as personal diaries and letters.

Annual Earnings. Average: $55,180. **Middle 50%:** $36,140–$79,800.

Employment Outlook. Workforce 2012: 3,800. **Projected Growth 2012–22:** 6.0%. **Projected Annual Openings**: 80.

Personality Type(s): Investigative. **Top Skills:** Science; Communication; Thought-Processing. **Work Environment:** Indoors; standing; walking and running; using hands; noisy; very bright or dim lighting; contaminants; cramped work space, awkward positions; minor burns, cuts, bites, or stings.

Typical Entry Requirements. Education: Master's degree (in History). **Work Experience:** None. **On-the-Job Training:** None.

Related Majors: History, p. 117.

HUMAN RESOURCES MANAGERS

Plan, direct, or coordinate human resources activities and staff of an organization.

Annual Earnings. Average: $100,800. **Middle 50%:** $76,750–$135,180.

Employment Outlook. Workforce 2012: 102,700. **Projected Growth 2012–22:** 13.2%. **Projected Annual Openings**: 4,060.

Personality Type(s): Enterprising–Social–Conventional. **Top Skills:** Management; Thought-Processing; Social; Technology/Programming; Mathematics; Communication. **Work Environment:** Indoors; sitting.

Typical Entry Requirements. Education: Bachelor's degree. **Work Experience:** 5 years or more. **On-the-Job Training:** None.

Related Majors: Human Resources Management, p. 77.

HUMAN RESOURCES SPECIALISTS

Perform activities in the human resource area. Includes employment specialists who screen, recruit, interview, and place workers.

Annual Earnings. Average: $56,630. **Middle 50%:** $42,470–$75,030.

Employment Outlook. Workforce 2012: 418,000. **Projected Growth 2012–22:** 7.9%. **Projected Annual Openings**: 10,950.

Personality Type(s): Enterprising–Conventional–Social. **Top Skills:** Social; Thought-Processing; Communication. **Work Environment:** Indoors; sitting; repetitive motions.

Typical Entry Requirements. Education: Bachelor's degree. **Work Experience:** None. **On-the-Job Training:** None.

Related Majors: Human Resources Management, p. 77.

HYDROLOGISTS

Research the distribution, circulation, and physical properties of underground and surface waters; and study the form and intensity of precipitation, its rate of infiltration into the soil, movement through the earth, and its return to the ocean and atmosphere.

Annual Earnings. Average: $75,710. **Middle 50%:** $61,220–$94,300.

Employment Outlook. Workforce 2012: 7,400. **Projected Growth 2012–22:** 10.4%. **Projected Annual Openings**: 290.

Personality Type(s): Investigative–Realistic. **Top Skills:** Science; Installation; Mathematics; Technology/Programming; Thought-Processing; Social; Communication; Equipment Use/Maintenance; Management. **Work Environment:** Indoors; outdoors; sitting.

Typical Entry Requirements. Education: Master's degree. **Work Experience:** None. **On-the-Job Training:** None.

Related Majors: Geology (or an engineering major), p. 113.

INDUSTRIAL ENGINEERS

Design, develop, test, and evaluate integrated systems for managing industrial production processes, including human work factors, quality control, inventory control, logistics and material flow, cost analysis, and production coordination.

Annual Earnings. Average: $80,300. **Middle 50%:** $64,760–$98,250.

Employment Outlook. Workforce 2012: 223,300. **Projected Growth 2012–22:** 4.5%. **Projected Annual Openings:** 7,540.

Personality Type(s): Investigative–Conventional–Enterprising. **Top Skills:** Mathematics; Thought-Processing; Technology/Programming; Social; Science; Management; Communication. **Work Environment:** Indoors; sitting; noisy; contaminants; hazardous equipment.

Typical Entry Requirements. Education: Bachelor's degree. **Work Experience:** None. **On-the-Job Training:** None.

Related Majors: Industrial Engineering, p. 106.

JOB SPECIALIZATION: HUMAN FACTORS ENGINEERS AND ERGONOMISTS

Design objects, facilities, and environments to optimize human well-being and overall system performance, applying theory, principles, and data regarding the relationship between humans and respective technology. Investigate and analyze characteristics of human behavior and performance as it relates to the use of technology.

Personality Type(s): Investigative–Realistic. **Top Skills:** Technology/Programming; Mathematics; Thought-Processing; Science; Communication; Social; Management. **Work Environment:** Indoors; sitting.

INDUSTRIAL PRODUCTION MANAGERS

Plan, direct, or coordinate the work activities and resources necessary for manufacturing products in accordance with cost, quality, and quantity specifications.

Annual Earnings. Average: $90,790. **Middle 50%:** $70,430–$118,090.

Employment Outlook. Workforce 2012: 172,700. **Projected Growth 2012–22:** -2.4%. **Projected Annual Openings:** 3,140.

Personality Type(s): Enterprising–Conventional. **Top Skills:** Thought-Processing; Management; Mathematics; Technology/Programming; Communication; Social; Equipment Use/Maintenance. **Work Environment:** Indoors; noisy.

Typical Entry Requirements. Education: Bachelor's degree. **Work Experience:** 5 years or more. **On-the-Job Training:** None.

Related Majors: Business Management and Administration, p. 74; Industrial Engineering, p. 106.

JOB SPECIALIZATION: BIOFUELS PRODUCTION MANAGERS

Manage biofuels production and plant operations. Collect and process information on plant production and performance, diagnose problems, and design corrective procedures.

Personality Type(s): Enterprising–Conventional–Realistic. **Top Skills:** No data available. **Work Environment:** No data available.

JOB SPECIALIZATION: BIOMASS POWER PLANT MANAGERS

Manage operations at biomass power generation facilities. Direct work activities at plant, including supervision of operations and maintenance staff.

Personality Type(s): Enterprising–Conventional–Realistic. **Top Skills:** Management; Equipment Use/Maintenance; Communication; Mathematics; Science; Social; Technology/Programming; Thought-Processing. **Work Environment:** Indoors; outdoors; sitting; noisy; very hot or cold; contaminants; heights; hazardous conditions; hazardous equipment.

JOB SPECIALIZATION: GEOTHERMAL PRODUCTION MANAGERS

Manage operations at geothermal power generation facilities. Maintain and monitor geothermal plant equipment for efficient and safe plant operations.

Personality Type(s): Enterprising–Conventional. **Top Skills:** Equipment Use/Maintenance; Management; Mathematics; Communication; Science; Social; Technology/Programming; Thought-Processing. **Work Environment:** Indoors; outdoors; sitting; noisy; very hot or cold; contaminants; hazardous conditions; hazardous equipment.

JOB SPECIALIZATION: HYDROELECTRIC PRODUCTION MANAGERS

Manage operations at hydroelectric power generation facilities. Maintain and monitor hydroelectric plant equipment for efficient and safe plant operations.

Personality Type(s): Enterprising–Conventional. **Top Skills:** No data available. **Work Environment:** No data available.

JOB SPECIALIZATION: METHANE/LANDFILL GAS COLLECTION SYSTEM OPERATORS

Direct daily operations, maintenance, or repair of landfill gas projects, including maintenance of daily logs, determination of service priorities, and compliance with reporting requirements.

Personality Type(s): Conventional–Enterprising–Realistic. **Top Skills:** No data available. **Work Environment:** No data available.

JOB SPECIALIZATION: QUALITY CONTROL SYSTEMS MANAGERS

Plan, direct, or coordinate quality assurance programs. Formulate quality control policies and control quality of laboratory and production efforts.

Personality Type(s): Enterprising–Conventional–Realistic. **Top Skills:** Management; Equipment Use/Maintenance; Technology/Programming; Social; Thought-Processing; Mathematics; Communication; Science. **Work Environment:** Indoors; outdoors; sitting; using hands; noisy; contaminants; hazardous conditions.

INDUSTRIAL-ORGANIZATIONAL PSYCHOLOGISTS

Apply principles of psychology to human resources, administration, management, sales, and marketing problems. Activities may include policy planning; employee testing and selection, training and development; and organizational development and analysis. May work with management to organize the work setting to improve worker productivity.

Annual Earnings. Average: $80,330. **Middle 50%:** $63,010–$107,490.

Employment Outlook. Workforce 2012: 1,600. **Projected Growth 2012–22:** 53.4%. **Projected Annual Openings**: 130.

Personality Type(s): Investigative–Enterprising–Artistic. **Top Skills:** Science; Mathematics; Communication; Thought-Processing; Technology/Programming; Social; Management. **Work Environment:** Indoors; sitting.

Typical Entry Requirements. Education: Master's degree (in Psychology). **Work Experience:** None. **On-the-Job Training:** Internship.

Related Majors: Psychology, p. 132.

INFORMATION SECURITY ANALYSTS

Plan, implement, upgrade, or monitor security measures for the protection of computer networks and information. May ensure appropriate security controls are in place that will safeguard digital files and vital electronic infrastructure. May respond to computer security breaches and viruses.

Annual Earnings. Average: $88,590. **Middle 50%:** $67,120–$113,100.

Employment Outlook. Workforce 2012: 75,100. **Projected Growth 2012–22:** 36.5%. **Projected Annual Openings**: 3,920.

Personality Type(s): Conventional–Investigative–Realistic. **Top Skills:** Installation; Thought-Processing; Technology/Programming; Social; Science; Communication; Management. **Work Environment:** Indoors; sitting; using hands.

Typical Entry Requirements. Education: Bachelor's degree. **Work Experience:** Less than 5 years. **On-the-Job Training:** None.

Related Majors: Computer Science, p. 85.

INSURANCE APPRAISERS, AUTO DAMAGE

Appraise automobile or other vehicle damage to determine repair costs for insurance claim settlement. Prepare insurance forms to indicate repair cost or cost estimates and recommendations. May seek agreement with automotive repair shop on repair costs.

Annual Earnings. Average: $61,660. **Middle 50%:** $52,410–$73,300.

Employment Outlook. Workforce 2012: 13,500. **Projected Growth 2012–22:** -5.3%. **Projected Annual Openings**: 310.

Personality Type(s): Conventional–Realistic–Enterprising. **Top Skills:** Communication; Mathematics. **Work Environment:** Indoors; outdoors; sitting; noisy; very hot or cold; contaminants.

Typical Entry Requirements. Education: Postsecondary non-degree award. **Work Experience:** None. **On-the-Job Training:** Moderate-term on-the-job training.

Related Majors: Risk Management and Insurance, p. 81.

INSURANCE SALES AGENTS

Sell life, property, casualty, health, automotive, or other types of insurance. May refer clients to independent brokers, work as an independent broker, or be employed by an insurance company.

Annual Earnings. Average: $48,210. **Middle 50%:** $34,230–$73,390.

Employment Outlook. Workforce 2012: 443,400. **Projected Growth 2012–22:** 10.4%. **Projected Annual Openings**: 15,020.

Personality Type(s): Enterprising–Conventional–Social. **Top Skills:** Mathematics; Communication; Social; Thought-Processing. **Work Environment:** Indoors; sitting.

Typical Entry Requirements. Education: High school diploma or equivalent. **Work Experience:** None. **On-the-Job Training:** Moderate-term on-the-job training.

Related Majors: Risk Management and Insurance, p. 81.

INSURANCE UNDERWRITERS

Review individual applications for insurance to evaluate degree of risk involved and determine acceptance of applications.

Annual Earnings. Average: $63,780. **Middle 50%:** $49,040–$85,640.

Employment Outlook. Workforce 2012: 106,300. **Projected Growth 2012–22:** -6.1%. **Projected Annual Openings**: 2,890.

Personality Type(s): Conventional–Enterprising–Investigative. **Top Skills:** Mathematics; Communication; Thought-Processing; Social. **Work Environment:** Indoors; sitting; repetitive motions.

Typical Entry Requirements. Education: Bachelor's degree. **Work Experience:** None. **On-the-Job Training:** Moderate-term on-the-job training.

Related Majors: Actuarial Science, p. 64; Risk Management and Insurance, p. 81.

INTERNISTS, GENERAL

Physicians who diagnose and provide non-surgical treatment of diseases and injuries of internal organ systems. Provide care mainly for adults who have a wide range of problems associated with the internal organs.

Annual Earnings. Average: $186,850. **Middle 50%:** $129,630–$187,200+.

Employment Outlook. Workforce 2012: 51,300. **Projected Growth 2012–22:** 14.1%. **Projected Annual Openings**: 2,010.

Personality Type(s): Investigative–Social–Realistic. **Top Skills:** Science; Communication; Thought-Processing; Social; Management; Mathematics. **Work Environment:** Indoors; standing; walking and running; using hands; disease or infections.

Typical Entry Requirements. Education: Professional degree (in Medicine). **Work Experience:** None. **On-the-Job Training:** Internship/ residency.

Related Majors: Pre-Professional Health (or any major, plus courses required for entry to medical school), p. 131.

INTERPRETERS AND TRANSLATORS

Interpret oral or sign language or translate written text from one language into another.

Annual Earnings. Average: $42,420. **Middle 50%:** $30,580–$58,930.

Employment Outlook. Workforce 2012: 63,600. **Projected Growth 2012–22:** 46.1%. **Projected Annual Openings**: 3,810.

Personality Type(s): Artistic–Social. **Top Skills:** Communication; Technology/Programming. **Work Environment:** Indoors; sitting; repetitive motions; noisy; disease or infections.

Typical Entry Requirements. Education: Bachelor's degree. **Work Experience:** None. **On-the-Job Training:** Short-term on-the-job training.

Related Majors: Modern Foreign Language, p. 124.

KINDERGARTEN TEACHERS, EXCEPT SPECIAL EDUCATION

Teach elemental natural and social science, personal hygiene, music, art, and literature to kindergarten students. Promote physical, mental, and social development. May be required to hold state certification.

Annual Earnings. Average: $50,230. **Middle 50%:** $40,620–$62,820.

Employment Outlook. Workforce 2012: 158,500. **Projected Growth 2012–22:** 13.0%. **Projected Annual Openings:** 6,510.

Personality Type(s): Social–Artistic. **Top Skills:** Social; Communication; Technology/Programming. **Work Environment:** Indoors; standing.

Typical Entry Requirements. Education: Bachelor's degree. **Work Experience:** None. **On-the-Job Training:** Student teaching.

Related Majors: Early Childhood Education (or a subject to be taught; see your state's requirements), p. 90.

LABOR RELATIONS SPECIALISTS

Resolve disputes between workers and managers, negotiate collective bargaining agreements, or coordinate grievance procedures to handle employee complaints.

Annual Earnings. Average: $54,630. **Middle 50%:** $21,020–$77,710.

Employment Outlook. Workforce 2012: 77,600. **Projected Growth 2012–22:** -0.8%. **Projected Annual Openings:** 1,420.

Personality Type(s): Enterprising–Conventional–Social

Typical Entry Requirements. Education: Bachelor's degree. **Work Experience:** None. **On-the-Job Training:** None.

Related Majors: Human Resources Management, p. 77.

LANDSCAPE ARCHITECTS

Plan and design land areas for projects such as parks and other recreational facilities, airports, highways, hospitals, schools, land subdivisions, and commercial, industrial, and residential sites.

Annual Earnings. Average: $64,790. **Middle 50%:** $48,860–$84,140.

Employment Outlook. Workforce 2012: 20,100. **Projected Growth 2012–22:** 14.3%. **Projected Annual Openings:** 760.

Personality Type(s): Artistic–Investigative–Realistic. **Top Skills:** Science; Thought-Processing; Technology/Programming; Mathematics; Management; Communication; Social. **Work Environment:** Indoors; outdoors; sitting.

Typical Entry Requirements. Education: Bachelor's degree. **Work Experience:** None. **On-the-Job Training:** Internship.

Related Majors: Landscape Architecture, p. 120.

LIFE SCIENTISTS, ALL OTHER

All life scientists not listed separately.

Annual Earnings. Average: $66,930. **Middle 50%:** $51,730–$92,740.

Employment Outlook. Workforce 2012: 9,900. **Projected Growth 2012–22:** 10.2%. **Projected Annual Openings:** 310.

Typical Entry Requirements. Education: Bachelor's degree. **Work Experience:** None. **On-the-Job Training:** None.

Related Majors: Biology, p. 71.

LOAN OFFICERS

Evaluate, authorize, or recommend approval of commercial, real estate, or credit loans. Advise borrowers on financial status and payment methods. Includes mortgage loan officers and agents, collection analysts, loan servicing officers, and loan underwriters.

Annual Earnings. Average: $61,420. **Middle 50%:** $44,030–$86,760.

Employment Outlook. Workforce 2012: 296,900. **Projected Growth 2012–22:** 7.7%. **Projected Annual Openings**: 7,720.

Personality Type(s): Conventional–Enterprising–Social. **Top Skills:** Communication; Social; Mathematics. **Work Environment:** Indoors; sitting.

Typical Entry Requirements. Education: Bachelor's degree. **Work Experience:** None. **On-the-Job Training:** Moderate-term on-the-job training.

Related Majors: Finance, p. 75.

LODGING MANAGERS

Plan, direct, or coordinate activities of an organization or department that provides lodging and other accommodations.

Annual Earnings. Average: $46,830. **Middle 50%:** $35,950–$65,630.

Employment Outlook. Workforce 2012: 50,400. **Projected Growth 2012–22:** 1.4%. **Projected Annual Openings**: 1,620.

Personality Type(s): Enterprising–Conventional–Social. **Top Skills:** Management; Social; Communication; Equipment Use/Maintenance; Thought-Processing; Mathematics. **Work Environment:** Indoors.

Typical Entry Requirements. Education: High school diploma or equivalent. **Work Experience:** Less than 5 years. **On-the-Job Training:** None.

Related Majors: Hospitality Management, p. 76.

MANAGEMENT ANALYSTS

Conduct organizational studies and evaluations, design systems and procedures, conduct work simplification and measurement studies, and prepare operations and procedures manuals to assist management in operating more efficiently and effectively. Includes program analysts and management consultants.

Annual Earnings. Average: $79,870. **Middle 50%:** $59,360–$106,950.

Employment Outlook. Workforce 2012: 718,700. **Projected Growth 2012–22:** 18.6%. **Projected Annual Openings**: 24,520.

Personality Type(s): Investigative–Enterprising–Conventional. **Top Skills:** Management; Thought-Processing; Social; Science; Mathematics; Communication. **Work Environment:** Indoors; sitting.

Typical Entry Requirements. Education: Bachelor's degree. **Work Experience:** Less than 5 years. **On-the-Job Training:** None.

Related Majors: Business Management and Administration, p. 74.

MANAGERS, ALL OTHER

All managers not listed separately.

Annual Earnings. Average: $103,530. **Middle 50%:** $75,050–$132,930.

Employment Outlook. Workforce 2012: 898,200. **Projected Growth 2012–22:** 5.9%. **Projected Annual Openings**: 24,910.

Typical Entry Requirements. Education: High school diploma or equivalent. **Work Experience:** Less than 5 years. **On-the-Job Training:** None.

Related Majors: Business Management and Administration, p. 74; Economics, p. 88.

JOB SPECIALIZATION: BROWNFIELD REDEVELOPMENT SPECIALISTS AND SITE MANAGERS

Plan and direct cleanup and redevelopment of contaminated properties for reuse. Does not include properties sufficiently contaminated to qualify as Superfund sites.

Personality Type(s): Enterprising–Investigative–Conventional. **Top Skills:** Management; Technology/Programming; Mathematics; Science; Communication; Social; Thought-Processing. **Work Environment:** Indoors; outdoors; sitting.

JOB SPECIALIZATION: COMPLIANCE MANAGERS

Plan, direct, or coordinate activities of an organization to ensure compliance with ethical or regulatory standards.

Personality Type(s): Conventional–Enterprising–Realistic. **Top Skills:** Social; Thought-Processing; Technology/Programming; Communication; Management. **Work Environment:** Indoors; sitting; repetitive motions.

JOB SPECIALIZATION: INVESTMENT FUND MANAGERS

Plan, direct, or coordinate investment strategy or operations for a large pool of liquid assets supplied by institutional investors or individual investors.

Personality Type(s): Enterprising–Conventional. **Top Skills:** Mathematics; Technology/Programming; Thought-Processing; Social; Management; Communication. **Work Environment:** Indoors; sitting.

JOB SPECIALIZATION: LOSS PREVENTION MANAGERS

Plan and direct policies, procedures, or systems to prevent the loss of assets. Determine risk exposure or potential liability and develop risk control measures.

Personality Type(s): Enterprising–Conventional. **Top Skills:** Management; Thought-Processing; Technology/Programming; Social; Mathematics; Communication. **Work Environment:** Indoors; standing.

JOB SPECIALIZATION: REGULATORY AFFAIRS MANAGERS

Plan, direct, or coordinate production activities of an organization to ensure compliance with regulations and standard operating procedures.

Personality Type(s): Enterprising–Conventional. **Top Skills:** Thought-Processing; Communication; Management; Social; Science. **Work Environment:** Indoors; sitting.

JOB SPECIALIZATION: SECURITY MANAGERS

Direct an organization's security functions, including physical security and safety of employees, facilities, and assets.

Personality Type(s): Enterprising–Conventional. **Top Skills:** Management; Technology/Programming; Social; Thought-Processing; Communication; Mathematics. **Work Environment:** Indoors; outdoors; sitting.

JOB SPECIALIZATION: SUPPLY CHAIN MANAGERS

Direct or coordinate production, purchasing, warehousing, distribution, or financial forecasting services or activities to limit costs and improve accuracy, customer service, or safety. Examine existing procedures or opportunities for streamlining activities to meet product distribution needs. Direct the movement, storage, or processing of inventory.

Personality Type(s): Enterprising–Conventional. **Top Skills:** Management; Thought-Processing; Social; Communication; Mathematics. **Work Environment:** Indoors; sitting.

JOB SPECIALIZATION: WIND ENERGY OPERATIONS MANAGERS

Manage wind field operations, including personnel, maintenance activities, financial activities, and planning.

Personality Type(s): Enterprising–Conventional–Realistic. **Top Skills:** No data available. **Work Environment:** No data available.

JOB SPECIALIZATION: WIND ENERGY PROJECT MANAGERS

Lead or manage the development and evaluation of potential wind energy business opportunities, including environmental studies, permitting, and proposals. May also manage construction of projects.

Personality Type(s): Enterprising–Conventional–Investigative. **Top Skills:** No data available. **Work Environment:** No data available.

MARKET RESEARCH ANALYSTS AND MARKETING SPECIALISTS

Research market conditions in local, regional, or national areas; gather information to determine potential sales of a product or service; or create a marketing campaign. May gather information on competitors, prices, sales, and methods of marketing and distribution.

Annual Earnings. Average: $60,800. **Middle 50%:** $44,110–$85,310.

Employment Outlook. Workforce 2012: 415,700. **Projected Growth 2012–22:** 31.6%. **Projected Annual Openings**: 18,850.

Personality Type(s): Investigative–Enterprising–Conventional. **Top Skills:** Management; Mathematics; Science; Social; Technology/ Programming; Thought-Processing; Communication. **Work Environment:** Indoors; sitting.

Typical Entry Requirements. Education: Bachelor's degree. **Work Experience:** None. **On-the-Job Training:** None.

Related Majors: Marketing, p. 80.

MARKETING MANAGERS

Plan, direct, or coordinate marketing policies and programs, such as determining the demand for products and services offered by a firm and its competitors, and identify potential customers. Develop pricing strategies with the goal of maximizing the firm's profits or share of the market while ensuring the firm's customers are satisfied. Oversee product development or monitor trends that indicate the need for new products and services.

Annual Earnings. Average: $123,220. **Middle 50%:** $88,130–$166,250.

Employment Outlook. Workforce 2012: 180,500. **Projected Growth 2012–22:** 12.7%. **Projected Annual Openings:** 6,170.

Personality Type(s): Enterprising–Conventional. **Top Skills:** Management; Thought-Processing; Technology/Programming; Social; Mathematics; Communication; Science. **Work Environment:** Indoors; sitting.

Typical Entry Requirements. Education: Bachelor's degree. **Work Experience:** 5 years or more. **On-the-Job Training:** None.

Related Majors: Marketing, p. 80.

MARRIAGE AND FAMILY THERAPISTS

Diagnose and treat mental and emotional disorders, whether cognitive, affective, or behavioral, within the context of marriage and family systems. Apply psychotherapeutic and family systems theories and techniques in the delivery of services to individuals, couples, and families for the purpose of treating such diagnosed nervous and mental disorders.

Annual Earnings. Average: $48,160. **Middle 50%:** $37,080–$63,210.

Employment Outlook. Workforce 2012: 37,800. **Projected Growth 2012–22:** 30.6%. **Projected Annual Openings**: 1,960.

Personality Type(s): Social–Artistic–Investigative. **Top Skills:** Science; Social; Communication; Thought-Processing. **Work Environment:** Indoors; sitting.

Typical Entry Requirements. Education: Master's degree (in Counseling, Marriage and Family Therapy, Psychology, or Social Work). **Work Experience:** None. **On-the-Job Training:** Internship.

Related Majors: Social Work (or any major, plus courses required for entry to master's program in social work), p. 136.

MATERIALS ENGINEERS

Evaluate materials and develop machinery and processes to manufacture materials for use in products that must meet specialized design and performance specifications. Develop new uses for known materials. Includes those engineers working with composite materials or specializing in one type of material, such as graphite, metal and metal alloys, ceramics and glass, plastics and polymers, and naturally occurring materials. Includes metallurgists and metallurgical engineers, ceramic engineers, and welding engineers.

Annual Earnings. Average: $87,330. **Middle 50%:** $68,760–$110,550.

Employment Outlook. Workforce 2012: 23,200. **Projected Growth 2012–22:** 0.9%. **Projected Annual Openings**: 750.

Personality Type(s): Investigative–Realistic–Enterprising. **Top Skills:** Science; Mathematics; Technology/Programming; Thought-Processing; Communication; Management; Social. **Work Environment:** Indoors; sitting.

Typical Entry Requirements. Education: Bachelor's degree. **Work Experience:** None. **On-the-Job Training:** None.

Related Majors: Metallurgical Engineering, p. 108.

MATHEMATICAL SCIENCE OCCUPATIONS, ALL OTHER

All mathematical scientists not listed separately.

Annual Earnings. Average: $60,820. **Middle 50%:** $43,610–$85,470.

Employment Outlook. Workforce 2012: 1,900. **Projected Growth 2012–22:** 13.3%. **Projected Annual Openings:** 70.

Personality Type(s): No data available. **Top Skills:** No data available. **Work Environment:** No data available.

Typical Entry Requirements. Education: Bachelor's degree. **Work Experience:** None. **On-the-Job Training:** None.

Related Majors: Mathematics, p. 122.

MATHEMATICIANS

Conduct research in fundamental mathematics or in application of mathematical techniques to science, management, and other fields. Solve problems in various fields using mathematical methods.

Annual Earnings. Average: $102,440. **Middle 50%:** $72,170–$128,590.

Employment Outlook. Workforce 2012: 3,500. **Projected Growth 2012–22:** 22.7%. **Projected Annual Openings:** 170.

Personality Type(s): Investigative–Conventional–Artistic. **Top Skills:** Science; Mathematics; Communication; Thought-Processing. **Work Environment:** Indoors; sitting.

Typical Entry Requirements. Education: Master's degree (in Mathematics). **Work Experience:** None. **On-the-Job Training:** None.

Related Majors: Mathematics, p. 122.

MECHANICAL ENGINEERS

Perform engineering duties in planning and designing tools, engines, machines, and other mechanically functioning equipment. Oversee installation, operation, maintenance, and repair of equipment such as centralized heat, gas, water, and steam systems.

Annual Earnings. Average: $82,100. **Middle 50%:** $65,370–$102,770.

Employment Outlook. Workforce 2012: 258,100. **Projected Growth 2012–22:** 4.5%. **Projected Annual Openings:** 9,970.

Personality Type(s): Investigative–Realistic–Conventional. **Top Skills:** Science; Technology/Programming; Mathematics; Installation; Management; Equipment Use/Maintenance; Thought-Processing; Communication; Social. **Work Environment:** Indoors; sitting; noisy.

Typical Entry Requirements. Education: Bachelor's degree. **Work Experience:** None. **On-the-Job Training:** None.

Related Majors: Mechanical Engineering, p. 107.

JOB SPECIALIZATION: AUTOMOTIVE ENGINEERS

Develop new or improved designs for vehicle structural members, engines, transmissions, or other vehicle systems, using computer-assisted design technology. Direct building, modification, or testing of vehicle or components.

Personality Type(s): Realistic–Investigative. **Top Skills:** Science; Technology/Programming; Mathematics; Thought-Processing; Social; Equipment Use/Maintenance; Communication; Management. **Work Environment:** Indoors; sitting.

JOB SPECIALIZATION: FUEL CELL ENGINEERS

Design, evaluate, modify, or construct fuel cell components or systems for transportation, stationary, or portable applications.

Personality Type(s): Realistic–Investigative. **Top Skills:** Science; Technology/Programming; Mathematics; Equipment Use/Maintenance; Installation; Communication; Social; Thought-Processing; Management. **Work Environment:** Indoors; sitting.

MEDICAL AND CLINICAL LABORATORY TECHNOLOGISTS

Perform complex medical laboratory tests for diagnosis, treatment, and prevention of disease. May train or supervise staff.

Annual Earnings. Average: $58,430. **Middle 50%:** $49,100–$69,900.

Employment Outlook. Workforce 2012: 164,300. **Projected Growth 2012–22:** 13.8%. **Projected Annual Openings**: 6,580.

Personality Type(s): Investigative–Realistic–Conventional. **Top Skills:** Science; Equipment Use/Maintenance; Management; Thought-Processing; Social; Mathematics; Communication. **Work Environment:** Indoors; standing; using hands; repetitive motions; contaminants; disease or infections; hazardous conditions.

Typical Entry Requirements. Education: Bachelor's degree. **Work Experience:** None. **On-the-Job Training:** None.

Related Majors: Medical Technology, p. 123.

JOB SPECIALIZATION: CYTOGENETIC TECHNOLOGISTS

Analyze chromosomes found in biological specimens such as amniotic fluids, bone marrow, and blood to aid in the study, diagnosis, or treatment of genetic diseases.

Personality Type(s): Investigative–Realistic–Conventional. **Top Skills:** Science; Thought-Processing; Communication; Mathematics. **Work Environment:** Indoors; sitting; using hands; repetitive motions; disease or infections; hazardous conditions.

JOB SPECIALIZATION: CYTOTECHNOLOGISTS

Stain, mount, and study cells to detect evidence of cancer, hormonal abnormalities, and other pathological conditions following established standards and practices.

Personality Type(s): Investigative–Realistic. **Top Skills:** Science; Mathematics; Communication; Equipment Use/Maintenance. **Work Environment:** Indoors; sitting; using hands; repetitive motions; disease or infections; hazardous conditions.

JOB SPECIALIZATION: HISTOTECHNOLOGISTS AND HISTOLOGIC TECHNICIANS

Prepare histologic slides from tissue sections for microscopic examination and diagnosis by pathologists. May assist in research studies.

Personality Type(s): Realistic–Investigative–Conventional. **Top Skills:** Equipment Use/Maintenance; Science; Technology/Programming; Management; Mathematics. **Work Environment:** Indoors; sitting; using hands; repetitive motions; contaminants; disease or infections; hazardous conditions; hazardous equipment.

MEDICAL AND HEALTH SERVICES MANAGERS

Plan, direct, or coordinate medical and health services in hospitals, clinics, managed care organizations, public health agencies, or similar organizations.

Annual Earnings. Average: $90,940. **Middle 50%:** $70,960–$117,740.

Employment Outlook. Workforce 2012: 315,500. **Projected Growth 2012–22:** 23.2%. **Projected Annual Openings:** 14,990.

Personality Type(s): Enterprising–Conventional–Social. **Top Skills:** Management; Science; Mathematics; Social; Thought-Processing;

Communication. **Work Environment:** Indoors; sitting; disease or infections.

Typical Entry Requirements. Education: Bachelor's degree. **Work Experience:** None. **On-the-Job Training:** None.

Related Majors: Health Facilities Administration, p. 116.

MENTAL HEALTH AND SUBSTANCE ABUSE SOCIAL WORKERS

Assess and treat individuals with mental, emotional, or substance abuse problems, including abuse of alcohol, tobacco, and other drugs. Activities may include individual and group therapy, crisis intervention, case management, client advocacy, prevention, and education.

Annual Earnings. Average: $40,970. **Middle 50%:** $32,160–$53,830.

Employment Outlook. Workforce 2012: 114,200. **Projected Growth 2012–22:** 22.8%. **Projected Annual Openings:** 5,020.

Personality Type(s): Social–Investigative–Artistic. **Top Skills:** Science; Social; Communication; Thought-Processing. **Work Environment:** Indoors; sitting.

Typical Entry Requirements. Education: Bachelor's degree. **Work Experience:** None. **On-the-Job Training:** None.

Related Majors: Social Work, p. 136.

MIDDLE SCHOOL TEACHERS, EXCEPT SPECIAL AND CAREER/ TECHNICAL EDUCATION

Teach students in one or more subjects in public or private schools at the middle, intermediate, or junior high level, which falls between elementary and senior high school as defined by applicable laws and regulations.

Annual Earnings. Average: $53,940. **Middle 50%:** $43,790–$67,420.

Employment Outlook. Workforce 2012: 614,400. **Projected Growth 2012–22:** 12.4%. **Projected Annual Openings**: 21,120.

Personality Type(s): Social–Artistic. **Top Skills:** Mathematics; Social; Communication; Thought-Processing. **Work Environment:** Indoors; standing; noisy.

Typical Entry Requirements. Education: Bachelor's degree. **Work Experience:** None. **On-the-Job Training:** Student teaching.

Related Majors: Elementary Education, p. 91; Family and Consumer Sciences Education, p. 92; Physical Education (or a subject to be taught; see your state's requirements), p. 93.

MULTIMEDIA ARTISTS AND ANIMATORS

Create special effects, animation, or other visual images using film, video, computers, or other electronic tools and media for use in products or creations, such as computer games, movies, music videos, and commercials.

Annual Earnings. Average: $64,470. **Middle 50%:** $46,590–$88,750.

Employment Outlook. Workforce 2012: 68,900. **Projected Growth 2012–22:** 6.3%. **Projected Annual Openings**: 2,060.

Personality Type(s): Artistic–Investigative. **Top Skills:** Social; Technology/Programming; Thought-Processing; Management; Communication. **Work Environment:** Indoors; sitting; using hands; repetitive motions.

Typical Entry Requirements. Education: Bachelor's degree. **Work Experience:** None. **On-the-Job Training:** Moderate-term on-the-job training.

Related Majors: Graphic Design, p. 114.

MUSEUM TECHNICIANS AND CONSERVATORS

Restore, maintain, or prepare objects in museum collections for storage, research, or exhibit. May work with specimens, such as fossils, skeletal parts, or botanicals, or artifacts, textiles, or art. May identify and record objects or install and arrange them in exhibits. Includes book or document conservators.

Annual Earnings. Average: $40,020. **Middle 50%:** $31,200–$54,050.

Employment Outlook. Workforce 2012: 11,300. **Projected Growth 2012–22:** 7.1%. **Projected Annual Openings:** 330.

Personality Type(s): Realistic–Artistic. **Top Skills:** Installation; Communication; Technology/Programming; Science. **Work Environment:** Indoors; sitting; using hands; noisy; contaminants.

Typical Entry Requirements. Education: Bachelor's degree. **Work Experience:** None. **On-the-Job Training:** None.

Related Majors: Art History, p. 69.

NATURAL SCIENCES MANAGERS

Plan, direct, or coordinate activities in such fields as life sciences, physical sciences, mathematics, statistics, and research and development in these fields.

Annual Earnings. Average: $116,840. **Middle 50%:** $89,460–$160,470.

Employment Outlook. Workforce 2012: 51,600. **Projected Growth 2012–22:** 5.7%. **Projected Annual Openings:** 1,370.

Personality Type(s): Enterprising–Investigative. **Top Skills:** Science; Technology/Programming; Thought-Processing; Management; Communication; Mathematics; Social. **Work Environment:** Indoors; sitting; noisy; contaminants.

Typical Entry Requirements. Education: Bachelor's degree. **Work Experience:** 5 years or more. **On-the-Job Training:** None.

Related Majors: Biology, p. 71; Chemistry, p. 83; Geology, p. 113; Mathematics, p. 122; Physics, p. 128; Statistics, p. 139.

JOB SPECIALIZATION: CLINICAL RESEARCH COORDINATORS

Plan, direct, or coordinate clinical research projects. Direct the activities of workers engaged in clinical research projects to ensure compliance with protocols and overall clinical objectives. May evaluate and analyze clinical data.

Personality Type(s): Enterprising–Investigative–Conventional. **Top Skills:** Management; Science; Thought-Processing; Technology/ Programming; Social; Mathematics; Communication. **Work Environment:** Indoors; sitting.

JOB SPECIALIZATION: WATER RESOURCE SPECIALISTS

Design or implement programs and strategies related to water resource issues such as supply, quality, and regulatory compliance issues.

Personality Type(s): Investigative–Enterprising–Conventional. **Top Skills:** Mathematics; Science; Management; Social; Communication; Technology/Programming; Thought-Processing. **Work Environment:** Indoors; outdoors; sitting.

OBSTETRICIANS AND GYNECOLOGISTS

Physicians who provide medical care related to pregnancy or childbirth and those who diagnose, treat, and help prevent diseases of women, particularly those affecting the reproductive system. May also provide general medical care to women.

Annual Earnings. Average: No data available. **Middle 50%:** No data available.

Employment Outlook. Workforce 2012: 23,600. **Projected Growth 2012–22:** 14.4%. **Projected Annual Openings**: 930.

Personality Type(s): Investigative–Social–Realistic. **Top Skills:** Science; Communication; Thought-Processing; Mathematics; Management; Social. **Work Environment:** Indoors; standing; using hands; disease or infections.

Typical Entry Requirements. Education: Professional degree (in Medicine). **Work Experience:** None. **On-the-Job Training:** Internship/residency.

Related Majors: Pre-Professional Health (or any major, plus courses required for entry to medical school), p. 131.

OCCUPATIONAL THERAPISTS

Assess, plan, organize, and participate in rehabilitative programs that help build or restore vocational, homemaking, and daily living skills, as well as general independence, to persons with disabilities or developmental delays.

Annual Earnings. Average: $76,940. **Middle 50%:** $63,580–$91,600.

Employment Outlook. Workforce 2012: 113,200. **Projected Growth 2012–22:** 29.0%. **Projected Annual Openings**: 4,820.

Personality Type(s): Social–Investigative. **Top Skills:** Science; Thought-Processing; Technology/Programming; Social; Management; Communication. **Work Environment:** Indoors; using hands; disease or infections.

Typical Entry Requirements. Education: Master's degree (in Occupational Therapy). **Work Experience:** None. **On-the-Job Training:** None.

Related Majors: Pre-Professional Health (or any major, plus courses required for entry to graduate program in occupational therapy), p. 131.

JOB SPECIALIZATION: LOW VISION THERAPISTS, ORIENTATION AND MOBILITY SPECIALISTS, AND VISION REHABILITATION THERAPISTS

Provide therapy to patients with visual impairments to improve their functioning in daily life activities. May train patients in activities such as computer use, communication skills, or home management skills.

Personality Type(s): Social–Investigative–Realistic. **Top Skills:** Technology/Programming; Social; Communication; Thought-Processing. **Work Environment:** Outdoors; indoors; standing; walking and running; very hot or cold.

OPTOMETRISTS

Diagnose, manage, and treat conditions and diseases of the human eye and visual system. Examine eyes and visual system, diagnose problems or impairments, prescribe corrective lenses, and provide treatment. May prescribe therapeutic drugs to treat specific eye conditions.

Annual Earnings. Average: $101,290. **Middle 50%:** $76,720–$132,100.

Employment Outlook. Workforce 2012: 33,100. **Projected Growth 2012–22:** 24.4%. **Projected Annual Openings**: 1,770.

Personality Type(s): Investigative–Social–Realistic. **Top Skills:** Science; Communication; Social; Technology/Programming; Thought-Processing; Management; Mathematics. **Work Environment:** Indoors; sitting; using hands; repetitive motions; disease or infections.

Typical Entry Requirements. Education: Professional degree (in Optometry). **Work Experience:** None. **On-the-Job Training:** None.

Related Majors: Pre-Professional Health (or any major, plus courses required for entry to optometry school), p. 131.

ORAL AND MAXILLOFACIAL SURGEONS

Perform surgery and related procedures on the hard and soft tissues of the oral and maxillofacial regions to treat diseases, injuries, or defects. May diagnose problems of the oral and maxillofacial regions. May perform surgery to improve function or appearance.

Annual Earnings. Average: No data available. **Middle 50%:** No data available.

Employment Outlook. Workforce 2012: 6,700. **Projected Growth 2012–22:** 16.1%. **Projected Annual Openings**: 270.

Personality Type(s): Realistic–Social–Investigative. **Top Skills:** Science; Management; Thought-Processing; Technology/Programming; Social; Mathematics; Communication; Equipment Use/Maintenance. **Work Environment:** Indoors; standing; using hands; bending or twisting body; repetitive motions; contaminants; radiation; disease or infections.

Typical Entry Requirements. Education: Professional degree (in Dentistry). **Work Experience:** None. **On-the-Job Training:** Residency.

Related Majors: Pre-Professional Health (or any major, plus courses required for entry to dentistry school), p. 131.

ORTHODONTISTS

Examine, diagnose, and treat dental malocclusions and oral cavity anomalies. Design and fabricate appliances to realign teeth and jaws to produce and maintain normal function and to improve appearance.

Annual Earnings. Average: No data available. **Middle 50%:** No data available.

Employment Outlook. Workforce 2012: 7,500. **Projected Growth 2012–22:** 16.3%. **Projected Annual Openings**: 300.

Personality Type(s): Investigative–Realistic–Social. **Top Skills:** Science; Technology/Programming; Social; Management; Communication;

Thought-Processing. **Work Environment:** Indoors; sitting; using hands; repetitive motions; disease or infections.

Typical Entry Requirements. Education: Professional degree (in Dentistry). **Work Experience:** None. **On-the-Job Training:** Residency.

Related Majors: Pre-Professional Health (or any major, plus courses required for entry to dentistry school), p. 131.

PEDIATRICIANS, GENERAL

Physicians who diagnose, treat, and help prevent children's diseases and injuries.

Annual Earnings. Average: $157,610. **Middle 50%:** $125,850–$187,200+.

Employment Outlook. Workforce 2012: 34,700. **Projected Growth 2012–22:** 15.7%. **Projected Annual Openings:** 1,410.

Personality Type(s): Investigative–Social. **Top Skills:** Science; Thought-Processing; Social; Management; Communication. **Work Environment:** Indoors; standing; disease or infections.

Typical Entry Requirements. Education: Professional degree (in Medicine). **Work Experience:** None. **On-the-Job Training:** Internship/ residency.

Related Majors: Pre-Professional Health (or any major, plus courses required for entry to medical school), p. 131.

PERSONAL FINANCIAL ADVISORS

Advise clients on financial plans using knowledge of tax and investment strategies, securities, insurance, pension plans, and real estate. Duties include assessing clients' assets, liabilities, cash flow, insurance coverage, tax status, and financial objectives.

Annual Earnings. Average: $75,320. **Middle 50%:** $49,410–$124,680.

Employment Outlook. Workforce 2012: 223,400. **Projected Growth 2012–22:** 27.0%. **Projected Annual Openings**: 9,640.

Personality Type(s): Enterprising–Conventional–Social. **Top Skills:** Mathematics; Social; Thought-Processing; Communication; Management. **Work Environment:** Indoors; sitting.

Typical Entry Requirements. Education: Bachelor's degree. **Work Experience:** None. **On-the-Job Training:** None.

Related Majors: Finance, p. 75.

PETROLEUM ENGINEERS

Devise methods to improve oil and gas extraction and production and determine the need for new or modified tool designs. Oversee drilling and offer technical advice.

Annual Earnings. Average: $132,320. **Middle 50%:** $98,390–$186,520.

Employment Outlook. Workforce 2012: 38,500. **Projected Growth 2012–22:** 25.5%. **Projected Annual Openings**: 1,960.

Personality Type(s): Investigative–Realistic–Conventional. **Top Skills:** Science; Technology/Programming; Management; Mathematics; Thought-Processing; Social; Communication; Equipment Use/Maintenance; Installation. **Work Environment:** Indoors; sitting.

Typical Entry Requirements. Education: Bachelor's degree. **Work Experience:** None. **On-the-Job Training:** None.

Related Majors: Petroleum Engineering, p. 110.

PHARMACISTS

Dispense drugs prescribed by physicians and other health practitioners and provide information to patients about medications and their use. May advise physicians and other health practitioners on the selection, dosage, interactions, and side effects of medications.

Annual Earnings. Average: $119,280. **Middle 50%:** $104,400–$136,360.

Employment Outlook. Workforce 2012: 286,400. **Projected Growth 2012–22:** 14.5%. **Projected Annual Openings**: 10,980.

Personality Type(s): Investigative–Conventional–Social. **Top Skills:** Science; Social; Communication; Thought-Processing; Management; Mathematics. **Work Environment:** Indoors; standing; using hands; repetitive motions; noisy; disease or infections.

Typical Entry Requirements. Education: Professional degree (in Pharmacy). **Work Experience:** None. **On-the-Job Training:** None.

Related Majors: Pre-Professional Health (or any major, plus courses required for entry to pharmacy school), p. 131.

PHILOSOPHY AND RELIGION TEACHERS, POSTSECONDARY

Teach courses in philosophy, religion, and theology. Includes both teachers primarily engaged in teaching and those who do a combination of teaching and research.

Annual Earnings. Average: $65,540. **Middle 50%:** $49,110–$88,990.

Employment Outlook. Workforce 2012: 30,800. **Projected Growth 2012–22:** 19.3%. **Projected Annual Openings**: 1,060.

Personality Type(s): Social–Artistic–Investigative. **Top Skills:** Communication; Science; Thought-Processing; Social. **Work Environment:** Indoors; sitting.

Typical Entry Requirements. Education: Doctoral degree (in Philosophy or Religion). **Work Experience:** None. **On-the-Job Training:** None.

Related Majors: Philosophy, p. 127.

PHYSICAL THERAPISTS

Assess, plan, organize, and participate in rehabilitative programs that improve mobility, relieve pain, increase strength, and improve or correct disabling conditions resulting from disease or injury.

Annual Earnings. Average: $81,030. **Middle 50%:** $67,700–$93,820.

Employment Outlook. Workforce 2012: 204,200. **Projected Growth 2012–22:** 36.0%. **Projected Annual Openings**: 12,370.

Personality Type(s): Social–Investigative–Realistic. **Top Skills:** Science; Thought-Processing; Technology/Programming; Social; Management; Communication. **Work Environment:** Indoors; standing; using hands; disease or infections.

Typical Entry Requirements. Education: Professional degree (in Physical Therapy). **Work Experience:** None. **On-the-Job Training:** None.

Related Majors: Pre-Professional Health (or any major, plus courses required for entry to graduate program in physical therapy), p. 131.

PHYSICIAN ASSISTANTS

Provide health-care services typically performed by a physician, under the supervision of a physician. Conduct complete physicals, provide treatment, and counsel patients. May, in some cases, prescribe medication. Must graduate from an accredited educational program for physician assistants.

Annual Earnings. Average: $92,970. **Middle 50%:** $79,820–$111,430.

Employment Outlook. Workforce 2012: 86,700. **Projected Growth 2012–22:** 38.4%. **Projected Annual Openings**: 4,890.

Personality Type(s): Social–Investigative–Realistic. **Top Skills:** Science; Communication; Thought-Processing; Mathematics; Social. **Work Environment:** Indoors; standing; using hands; disease or infections.

Typical Entry Requirements. Education: Master's degree. **Work Experience:** None. **On-the-Job Training:** None.

Related Majors: Pre-Professional Health (or any science major), p. 131.

JOB SPECIALIZATION: ANESTHESIOLOGIST ASSISTANTS

Assist anesthesiologists in the administration of anesthesia for surgical and non-surgical procedures. Monitor patient status and provide patient care during surgical treatment.

Personality Type(s): Realistic–Social–Investigative. **Top Skills:** Science; Equipment Use/Maintenance; Installation; Management; Mathematics; Social; Technology/Programming; Thought-Processing; Communication. **Work Environment:** Indoors; standing; walking and running; using hands; repetitive motions; noisy; contaminants; radiation; disease or infections; hazardous conditions; minor burns, cuts, bites, or stings.

PHYSICIANS AND SURGEONS, ALL OTHER

All physicians and surgeons not listed separately.

Annual Earnings. Average: No data available. **Middle 50%:** No data available.

Employment Outlook. Workforce 2012: 348,900. **Projected Growth 2012–22:** 18.7%. **Projected Annual Openings**: 15,260.

Typical Entry Requirements. Education: Professional degree (in Medicine). **Work Experience:** None. **On-the-Job Training:** Internship/residency.

Related Majors: Pre-Professional Health (or any major, plus courses required for entry to medical school), p. 131.

JOB SPECIALIZATION: ALLERGISTS AND IMMUNOLOGISTS

Diagnose, treat, and help prevent allergic diseases and disease processes affecting the immune system.

Personality Type(s): Investigative–Social–Realistic. **Top Skills:** Science; Technology/Programming; Thought-Processing; Social; Management; Communication; Mathematics. **Work Environment:** Indoors; sitting; standing; disease or infections.

JOB SPECIALIZATION: DERMATOLOGISTS

Diagnose, treat, and help prevent diseases or other conditions of the skin.

Personality Type(s): Investigative–Social–Realistic. **Top Skills:** Science; Management; Social; Mathematics; Thought-Processing; Communication. **Work Environment:** Indoors; standing; using hands; contaminants; disease or infections; minor burns, cuts, bites, or stings.

JOB SPECIALIZATION: HOSPITALISTS

Provide inpatient care predominantly in settings such as medical wards, acute care units, intensive care units, rehabilitation centers, or emergency rooms. Manage and coordinate patient care throughout treatment.

Personality Type(s): Social–Investigative. **Top Skills:** Science; Social; Communication; Management; Mathematics; Thought-Processing. **Work Environment:** Indoors; noisy; disease or infections.

JOB SPECIALIZATION: NEUROLOGISTS

Diagnose, treat, and help prevent diseases and disorders of the nervous system.

Personality Type(s): Investigative–Social–Realistic. **Top Skills:** Science; Communication; Thought-Processing; Technology/Programming; Social; Management; Mathematics. **Work Environment:** Indoors; sitting; disease or infections.

JOB SPECIALIZATION: NUCLEAR MEDICINE PHYSICIANS

Diagnose and treat diseases using radioactive materials and techniques. May monitor radionuclide preparation, administration, and disposition.

Personality Type(s): Investigative–Social. **Top Skills:** Science; Thought-Processing; Communication; Mathematics; Management; Social. **Work Environment:** Indoors; sitting; radiation; disease or infections.

JOB SPECIALIZATION: OPHTHALMOLOGISTS

Diagnose, treat, and help prevent diseases and injuries of the eyes and related structures.

Personality Type(s): Investigative–Social–Realistic. **Top Skills:** Science; Communication; Technology/Programming; Social; Thought-Processing; Mathematics; Management. **Work Environment:** Indoors; sitting; using hands; repetitive motions; disease or infections

JOB SPECIALIZATION: PATHOLOGISTS

Diagnose presence and stage of diseases using laboratory techniques and patient specimens. Study the nature, cause, and development of diseases. May perform autopsies.

Personality Type(s): Investigative–Realistic. **Top Skills:** Science; Management; Communication; Social; Technology/Programming; Thought-Processing; Mathematics. **Work Environment:** Indoors; sitting; disease or infections.

JOB SPECIALIZATION: PHYSICAL MEDICINE AND REHABILITATION PHYSICIANS

Diagnose and treat disorders requiring physiotherapy to provide physical, mental, and occupational rehabilitation.

Personality Type(s): Investigative–Social–Realistic. **Top Skills:** Science; Technology/Programming; Thought-Processing; Mathematics;

Communication; Social; Management. **Work Environment:** Indoors; sitting; standing; using hands; disease or infections.

JOB SPECIALIZATION: PREVENTIVE MEDICINE PHYSICIANS

Apply knowledge of general preventive medicine and public health issues to promote health care to groups or individuals and aid in the prevention or reduction of risk of disease, injury, disability, or death. May practice population-based medicine or diagnose and treat patients in the context of clinical health promotion and disease prevention.

Personality Type(s): Social–Investigative–Realistic. **Top Skills:** Science; Thought-Processing; Social; Management; Communication; Technology/ Programming; Mathematics. **Work Environment:** Indoors; sitting; disease or infections.

JOB SPECIALIZATION: RADIOLOGISTS

Examine and diagnose disorders and diseases using X-rays and radioactive materials. May treat patients.

Personality Type(s): Investigative–Realistic–Social. **Top Skills:** Science; Management; Thought-Processing; Technology/Programming; Social; Mathematics; Communication. **Work Environment:** Indoors; sitting; using hands; radiation; disease or infections.

JOB SPECIALIZATION: SPORTS MEDICINE PHYSICIANS

Diagnose, treat, and help prevent injuries that occur during sporting events, athletic training, and physical activities.

Personality Type(s): Investigative–Social–Realistic. **Top Skills:** Science; Technology/Programming; Social; Management; Communication; Thought-Processing; Mathematics. **Work Environment:** Indoors; standing; using hands; disease or infections.

JOB SPECIALIZATION: UROLOGISTS

Diagnose, treat, and help prevent benign and malignant medical and surgical disorders of the genitourinary system and the renal glands.

Personality Type(s): Investigative–Social–Realistic. **Top Skills:** Science; Social; Thought-Processing; Communication; Management. **Work Environment:** Indoors; standing; using hands; contaminants; radiation; disease or infections.

PHYSICISTS

Conduct research into physical phenomena, develop theories on the basis of observation and experiments, and devise methods to apply physical laws and theories.

Annual Earnings. Average: $110,110. **Middle 50%:** $80,460–$142,880.

Employment Outlook. Workforce 2012: 20,600. **Projected Growth 2012–22:** 10.4%. **Projected Annual Openings**: 720.

Personality Type(s): Investigative–Realistic. **Top Skills:** Science; Mathematics; Technology/Programming; Thought-Processing; Communication; Social; Management. **Work Environment:** Indoors; sitting.

Typical Entry Requirements. Education: Doctoral or professional degree (in Physics). **Work Experience:** None. **On-the-Job Training:** None.

Related Majors: Physics, p. 128.

PODIATRISTS

Diagnose and treat diseases and deformities of the human foot.

Annual Earnings. Average: $118,210. **Middle 50%:** $82,050–$171,170.

Employment Outlook. Workforce 2012: 10,700. **Projected Growth 2012–22:** 22.5%. **Projected Annual Openings**: 460.

Personality Type(s): Investigative–Social–Realistic. **Top Skills:** Science; Communication; Technology/Programming; Management; Social;

Thought-Processing; Mathematics. **Work Environment:** Indoors; sitting; using hands; contaminants; radiation; disease or infections.

Typical Entry Requirements. Education: Professional degree (in Podiatry). **Work Experience:** None. **On-the-Job Training:** Internship/residency.

Related Majors: Pre-Professional Health (or any major, plus courses required for entry to podiatry school), p. 131.

POLITICAL SCIENTISTS

Study the origin, development, and operation of political systems. May study topics such as public opinion, political decision-making, and ideology. May analyze the structure and operation of governments, as well as various political entities. May conduct public opinion surveys, analyze election results, or analyze public documents.

Annual Earnings. Average: $100,920. **Middle 50%:** $71,420–$133,250.

Employment Outlook. Workforce 2012: 6,600. **Projected Growth 2012–22:** 21.3%. **Projected Annual Openings:** 250.

Personality Type(s): Investigative–Artistic–Social. **Top Skills:** Science; Communication; Thought-Processing; Social; Mathematics. **Work Environment:** Indoors; sitting.

Typical Entry Requirements. Education: Master's degree (in Political Science). **Work Experience:** None. **On-the-Job Training:** None.

Related Majors: Political Science, p. 129.

PRESCHOOL TEACHERS, EXCEPT SPECIAL EDUCATION

Instruct preschool-aged children in activities designed to promote social, physical, and intellectual growth needed for primary school in preschool, day-care center, or other child development facility.

Annual Earnings. Average: $27,570. **Middle 50%:** $21,660–$36,940.

Employment Outlook. Workforce 2012: 438,200. **Projected Growth 2012–22:** 17.4%. **Projected Annual Openings**: 19,940.

Personality Type(s): Social–Artistic. **Top Skills:** Social. **Work Environment:** Indoors; standing; noisy.

Typical Entry Requirements. Education: Associate's degree. **Work Experience:** None. **On-the-Job Training:** None.

Related Majors: Early Childhood Education (see your state's requirements), p. 90.

PROBATION OFFICERS AND CORRECTIONAL TREATMENT SPECIALISTS

Provide social services to assist in rehabilitation of law offenders in custody or on probation or parole. Make recommendations for actions involving formulation of rehabilitation plan and treatment of offender, including conditional release and education and employment stipulations.

Annual Earnings. Average: $48,440. **Middle 50%:** $37,590–$65,330.

Employment Outlook. Workforce 2012: 90,300. **Projected Growth 2012–22:** -1.0%. **Projected Annual Openings**: 2,360.

Personality Type(s): Social–Enterprising–Conventional. **Top Skills:** Social; Communication; Thought-Processing. **Work Environment:** Indoors; sitting; disease or infections.

Typical Entry Requirements. Education: Bachelor's degree. **Work Experience:** None. **On-the-Job Training:** Short-term on-the-job training.

Related Majors: Criminal Justice, p. 86; Psychology, p. 132; Social Work, p. 136.

PRODUCERS AND DIRECTORS

Produce or direct stage, television, radio, video, or motion picture productions for entertainment, information, or instruction. Responsible for creative decisions, such as interpretation of script, choice of actors or guests, set design, sound, special effects, and choreography.

Annual Earnings. Average: $69,480. **Middle 50%:** $45,070–$111,380.

Employment Outlook. Workforce 2012: 103,500. **Projected Growth 2012–22:** 2.8%. **Projected Annual Openings:** 3,790.

Typical Entry Requirements. Education: Bachelor's degree. **Work Experience:** Less than 5 years. **On-the-Job Training:** None.

Related Majors: Theater Arts, p. 141.

JOB SPECIALIZATION: DIRECTORS— STAGE, MOTION PICTURES, TELEVISION, AND RADIO

Interpret script, conduct rehearsals, and direct activities of cast and technical crew for stage, motion pictures, television, or radio programs.

Personality Type(s): Enterprising–Artistic. **Top Skills:** Management; Communication; Technology/Programming; Social. **Work Environment:** Indoors; sitting; using hands; repetitive motions; noisy.

JOB SPECIALIZATION: PRODUCERS

Plan and coordinate various aspects of radio, television, stage, or motion picture production, such as selecting script, coordinating writing, directing and editing, and arranging financing.

Personality Type(s): Enterprising–Artistic. **Top Skills:** Management; Social; Thought-Processing; Mathematics; Communication. **Work Environment:** Indoors; sitting.

JOB SPECIALIZATION: PROGRAM DIRECTORS

Direct and coordinate activities of personnel engaged in preparation of radio or television station program schedules and programs, such as sports or news.

Personality Type(s): Enterprising–Conventional–Artistic. **Top Skills:** Management; Communication; Social; Thought-Processing. **Work Environment:** Indoors; sitting; using hands.

JOB SPECIALIZATION: TALENT DIRECTORS

Audition and interview performers to select most appropriate talent for parts in stage, television, radio, or motion picture productions.

Personality Type(s): Enterprising–Artistic. **Top Skills:** Social; Communication; Thought-Processing; Management. **Work Environment:** Indoors; sitting; noisy.

JOB SPECIALIZATION: TECHNICAL DIRECTORS/MANAGERS

Coordinate activities of technical departments, such as taping, editing, engineering, and maintenance, to produce radio or television programs.

Personality Type(s): Enterprising–Realistic–Conventional. **Top Skills:** Technology/Programming; Social; Communication; Equipment Use/Maintenance; Management; Thought-Processing. **Work Environment:** Indoors; sitting; using hands.

PROSTHODONTISTS

Construct oral prostheses to replace missing teeth and other oral structures; to correct natural and acquired deformation of mouth and jaws; to restore and maintain oral function, such as chewing and speaking; and to improve appearance.

Annual Earnings. Average: $91,260. **Middle 50%:** $79,360–$179,980.

Employment Outlook. Workforce 2012: 400. **Projected Growth 2012–22:** 15.0%. **Projected Annual Openings**: 20.

Personality Type(s): Investigative–Realistic. **Top Skills:** Science; Technology/Programming; Thought-Processing; Social; Management; Equipment Use/Maintenance; Communication. **Work Environment:** Indoors; sitting; using hands; bending or twisting body; repetitive motions; noisy; contaminants; radiation; disease or infections; hazardous conditions; hazardous equipment.

Typical Entry Requirements. Education: Professional degree (in Dentistry). **Work Experience:** None. **On-the-Job Training:** Residency.

Related Majors: Pre-Professional Health (or any major, plus courses required for entry to dentistry school), p. 131.

PSYCHIATRISTS

Physicians who diagnose, treat, and help prevent disorders of the mind.

Annual Earnings. Average: $178,950. **Middle 50%:** $122,300–$187,200+.

Employment Outlook. Workforce 2012: 27,200. **Projected Growth 2012–22:** 16.2%. **Projected Annual Openings**: 1,120.

Personality Type(s): Investigative–Social–Artistic. **Top Skills:** Science; Communication; Thought-Processing; Social. **Work Environment:** Indoors; sitting; disease or infections.

Typical Entry Requirements. Education: Professional degree (in Medicine). **Work Experience:** None. **On-the-Job Training:** Internship/residency.

Related Majors: Pre-Professional Health (or any major, plus courses required for entry to medical school), p. 131.

PSYCHOLOGISTS, ALL OTHER

All psychologists not listed separately.

Annual Earnings. Average: $91,140. **Middle 50%:** $67,390–$104,880.

Employment Outlook. Workforce 2012: 13,400. **Projected Growth 2012–22:** 10.7%. **Projected Annual Openings:** 510.

Personality Type(s): No data available. **Top Skills:** No data available. **Work Environment:** No data available.

Typical Entry Requirements. Education: Master's degree (in Psychology). **Work Experience:** None. **On-the-Job Training:** Internship.

Related Majors: Psychology, p. 132.

JOB SPECIALIZATION: NEUROPSYCHOLOGISTS AND CLINICAL NEUROPSYCHOLOGISTS

Apply theories and principles of neuropsychology to diagnose and treat disorders of higher cerebral functioning.

Personality Type(s): Investigative–Social–Artistic. **Top Skills:** Science; Thought-Processing; Communication; Management; Mathematics; Social; Technology/Programming. **Work Environment:** Indoors; sitting; using hands; disease or infections.

PUBLIC RELATIONS AND FUNDRAISING MANAGERS

Plan, direct, or coordinate activities designed to create or maintain a favorable public image or raise issue awareness for their organization or client; or if engaged in fundraising, plan, direct, or coordinate activities to solicit and maintain funds for special projects or nonprofit organizations.

Annual Earnings. Average: $98,700. **Middle 50%:** $71,830–$137,710.

Employment Outlook. Workforce 2012: 62,100. **Projected Growth 2012–22:** 12.9%. **Projected Annual Openings:** 2,130.

Personality Type(s): Enterprising–Artistic. **Top Skills:** Management; Social; Thought-Processing; Mathematics; Communication. **Work Environment:** Indoors; sitting.

Typical Entry Requirements. Education: Bachelor's degree. **Work Experience:** 5 years or more. **On-the-Job Training:** None.

Related Majors: Communications, p. 84; English, p. 111; Journalism, p. 119; Public Relations, p. 134.

PUBLIC RELATIONS SPECIALISTS

Engage in promoting or creating an intended public image for individuals, groups, or organizations. May write or select material for release to various communications media.

Annual Earnings. Average: $54,940. **Middle 50%:** $40,290–$75,180.

Employment Outlook. Workforce 2012: 229,100. **Projected Growth 2012–22:** 12.0%. **Projected Annual Openings**: 5,880.

Personality Type(s): Enterprising–Artistic–Social. **Top Skills:** Social; Thought-Processing; Technology/Programming; Management; Communication. **Work Environment:** Indoors; sitting.

Typical Entry Requirements. Education: Bachelor's degree. **Work Experience:** None. **On-the-Job Training:** None.

Related Majors: Communication, p. 84; Public Relations (or a business major), p. 134.

RADIO AND TELEVISION ANNOUNCERS

Speak or read from scripted materials, such as news reports or commercial messages, on radio or television. May announce artist or title of performance, identify station, or interview guests.

Annual Earnings. Average: $29,020. **Middle 50%:** $20,000–$44,680.

Employment Outlook. Workforce 2012: 41,300. **Projected Growth 2012–22:** -0.1%. **Projected Annual Openings**: 860.

Personality Type(s): Artistic–Enterprising–Social. **Top Skills:** Communication; Social. **Work Environment:** Indoors; sitting; using hands.

Typical Entry Requirements. Education: Bachelor's degree. **Work Experience:** None. **On-the-Job Training:** None.

Related Majors: Communication, p. 84.

REGISTERED NURSES

Assess patient health problems and needs, develop and implement nursing care plans, and maintain medical records. Administer nursing care to ill, injured, convalescent, or disabled patients. May advise patients on health maintenance and disease prevention or provide case management. Licensing or registration required. Includes Clinical Nurse Specialists.

Annual Earnings. Average: $66,220. **Middle 50%:** $54,180–$80,190.

Employment Outlook. Workforce 2012: 2,711,500. **Projected Growth 2012–22:** 19.4%. **Projected Annual Openings**: 105,260.

Personality Type(s): Social–Investigative–Conventional. **Top Skills:** Science; Social; Communication; Thought-Processing; Management; Mathematics. **Work Environment:** Indoors; standing; walking and running; using hands; bending or twisting body; disease or infections.

Typical Entry Requirements. Education: Associate's or bachelor's degree. **Work Experience:** None. **On-the-Job Training:** None.

Related Majors: Nursing (RN Training), p. 125.

JOB SPECIALIZATION: ACUTE CARE NURSES

Provide advanced nursing care for patients with acute conditions such as heart attacks, respiratory distress syndrome, or shock. May care for pre-

and post-operative patients or perform advanced, invasive diagnostic or therapeutic procedures.

Personality Type(s): Social–Investigative–Realistic. **Top Skills:** Science; Thought-Processing; Social; Mathematics; Management; Communication; Technology/Programming. **Work Environment:** Indoors; standing; walking and running; using hands; noisy; contaminants; disease or infections.

JOB SPECIALIZATION: ADVANCED PRACTICE PSYCHIATRIC NURSES

Provide advanced nursing care for patients with psychiatric disorders. May provide psychotherapy under the direction of a psychiatrist.

Personality Type(s): Social–Investigative. **Top Skills:** Science; Management; Communication; Thought-Processing; Social. **Work Environment:** Indoors; sitting; disease or infections.

JOB SPECIALIZATION: CLINICAL NURSE SPECIALISTS

Plan, direct, or coordinate the daily patient care activities in a clinical practice. Ensure adherence to established clinical policies, protocols, regulations, and standards.

Personality Type(s): Enterprising–Social–Conventional. **Top Skills:** Science; Communication; Management; Mathematics; Social; Technology/Programming; Thought-Processing. **Work Environment:** Indoors; noisy; contaminants; disease or infections.

JOB SPECIALIZATION: CRITICAL CARE NURSES

Provide advanced nursing care for patients in critical or coronary care units.

Personality Type(s): Social–Investigative–Realistic. **Top Skills:** Science; Communication; Thought-Processing; Technology/Programming; Social;

Management; Mathematics. **Work Environment:** Indoors; standing; walking and running; using hands; bending or twisting body; noisy; contaminants; radiation; disease or infections.

RELIGIOUS WORKERS, ALL OTHER

All religious workers not listed separately.

Annual Earnings. Average: $28,750. **Middle 50%:** $19,790–$42,410.

Employment Outlook. Workforce 2012: 59,900. **Projected Growth 2012–22:** 8.9%. **Projected Annual Openings**: 1,910.

Typical Entry Requirements. Education: Bachelor's degree. **Work Experience:** None. **On-the-Job Training:** None.

Related Majors: Religious Studies, p. 135.

REPORTERS AND CORRESPONDENTS

Collect and analyze facts about newsworthy events by interview, investigation, or observation. Report and write stories for newspaper, news magazine, radio, or television.

Annual Earnings. Average: $35,600. **Middle 50%:** $26,500–$53,270.

Employment Outlook. Workforce 2012: 51,700. **Projected Growth 2012–22:** -13.8%. **Projected Annual Openings**: 1,760.

Personality Type(s): Artistic–Enterprising–Investigative. **Top Skills:** Communication; Social. **Work Environment:** Indoors; sitting.

Typical Entry Requirements. Education: Bachelor's degree. **Work Experience:** None. **On-the-Job Training:** None.

Related Majors: Communication, p. 84; Journalism, p. 119.

SALES MANAGERS

Plan, direct, or coordinate the actual distribution or movement of a product or service to the customer. Coordinate sales distribution by establishing sales territories, quotas, and goals and establish training programs for sales representatives. Analyze sales statistics gathered by staff to determine sales potential and inventory requirements and monitor the preferences of customers.

Annual Earnings. Average: $108,540. **Middle 50%:** $73,880–$155,090.

Employment Outlook. Workforce 2012: 359,300. **Projected Growth 2012–22:** 8.3%. **Projected Annual Openings**: 10,690.

Personality Type(s): Enterprising–Conventional. **Top Skills:** Management; Social; Thought-Processing; Technology/Programming; Communication; Mathematics. **Work Environment:** Indoors; sitting.

Typical Entry Requirements. Education: Bachelor's degree. **Work Experience:** Less than 5 years. **On-the-Job Training:** None.

Related Majors: Business Management and Administration, p. 74; Marketing, p. 80.

SECONDARY SCHOOL TEACHERS, EXCEPT SPECIAL AND CAREER/ TECHNICAL EDUCATION

Teach students in one or more subjects, such as English, mathematics, or social studies at the secondary level in public or private schools. May be designated according to subject matter specialty.

Annual Earnings. Average: $55,360. **Middle 50%:** $44,440–$69,970.

Employment Outlook. Workforce 2012: 955,800. **Projected Growth 2012–22:** 5.5%. **Projected Annual Openings**: 31,260.

Personality Type(s): Social–Artistic–Enterprising. **Top Skills:** Science; Technology/Programming; Thought-Processing; Social; Management; Communication; Mathematics. **Work Environment:** Indoors; standing.

Typical Entry Requirements. Education: Bachelor's degree. **Work Experience:** None. **On-the-Job Training:** Student teaching.

Related Majors: Biology, p. 71; Chemistry, p. 83; English, p. 111; Family and Consumer Sciences Education, p. 92; History, p. 117; Mathematics, p. 122; Modern Foreign Language, p. 124; Physical Education, p. 93; Physics, p. 128; Secondary Education (or another subject to be taught; see your state's requirements), p. 94.

SOCIAL AND COMMUNITY SERVICE MANAGERS

Plan, direct, or coordinate the activities of a social service program or community outreach organization. Oversee the program or organization's budget and policies regarding participant involvement, program requirements, and benefits. Work may involve directing social workers, counselors, or probation officers.

Plan, direct, or coordinate the activities of a social service program or community outreach organization. Oversee the program or organization's budget and policies regarding participant involvement, program requirements, and benefits. Work may involve directing social workers, counselors, or probation officers.

Annual Earnings. Average: $61,160. **Middle 50%:** $46,680–$79,150.

Employment Outlook. Workforce 2012: 132,900. **Projected Growth 2012–22:** 20.8%. **Projected Annual Openings:** 5,510.

Personality Type(s): Enterprising–Social. **Top Skills:** Management; Thought-Processing; Social; Science; Mathematics; Communication. **Work Environment:** Indoors; sitting.

Typical Entry Requirements. Education: Bachelor's degree. **Work Experience:** 5 years or more. **On-the-Job Training:** None.

Related Majors: Business Management and Administration, p. 74; Social Work, p. 136.

SOCIAL WORK TEACHERS, POSTSECONDARY

Teach courses in social work. Includes both teachers primarily engaged in teaching and those who do a combination of teaching and research.

Annual Earnings. Average: $64,280. **Middle 50%:** $48,140–$88,810.

Employment Outlook. Workforce 2012: 12,400. **Projected Growth 2012–22:** 13.1%. **Projected Annual Openings:** 350.

Personality Type(s): Social–Investigative. **Top Skills:** Communication; Mathematics; Thought-Processing; Science; Management; Social. **Work Environment:** Indoors; sitting.

Typical Entry Requirements. Education: Doctoral degree (in Social Work). **Work Experience:** None. **On-the-Job Training:** None.

Related Majors: Social Work, p. 136.

SOCIAL WORKERS, ALL OTHER

All social workers not listed separately.

Annual Earnings. Average: $72,430. **Middle 50%:** $53,650–$94,570.

Employment Outlook. Workforce 2012: 2,600. **Projected Growth 2012–22:** 15.0%. **Projected Annual Openings:** 110.

Personality Type(s): Investigative–Artistic–Social. **Top Skills:** Science; Communication; Management; Mathematics; Social; Thought-Processing. **Work Environment:** Indoors; sitting.

Typical Entry Requirements. Education: Master's degree (in Sociology). **Work Experience:** None. **On-the-Job Training:** None.

Related Majors: Social Work, p. 136.

SOCIOLOGISTS

Study human society and social behavior by examining the groups and social institutions that people form, as well as various social, religious, political, and business organizations. May study the behavior and interaction of groups, trace their origin and growth, and analyze the influence of group activities on individual members.

Annual Earnings. Average: $72,430. **Middle 50%:** $53,650–$94,570.

Employment Outlook. Workforce 2012: 2,600. **Projected Growth 2012–22:** 15.0%. **Projected Annual Openings:** 110.

Personality Type(s): Investigative–Artistic–Social. **Top Skills:** Science; Communication; Management; Mathematics; Social; Thought-Processing. **Work Environment:** Indoors; sitting.

Typical Entry Requirements. Education: Master's degree (in Sociology). **Work Experience:** None. **On-the-Job Training:** None.

Related Majors: Sociology, p. 138.

SOFTWARE DEVELOPERS, APPLICATIONS

Develop, create, and modify general computer applications software or specialized utility programs. Analyze user needs and develop software solutions. Design software or customize software for client use with the aim of optimizing operational efficiency. May analyze and design databases within an application area, working individually or coordinating database development as part of a team. May supervise computer programmers.

Annual Earnings. Average: $92,660. **Middle 50%:** $72,290–$116,630.

Employment Outlook. Workforce 2012: 613,000. **Projected Growth 2012–22:** 22.8%. **Projected Annual Openings:** 21,850.

Personality Type(s): Investigative–Realistic–Conventional. **Top Skills:** Technology/Programming; Mathematics; Thought-Processing; Science;

Installation; Communication; Social; Equipment Use/Maintenance; Management. **Work Environment:** Indoors; sitting; repetitive motions.

Typical Entry Requirements. Education: Bachelor's degree. **Work Experience:** None. **On-the-Job Training:** None.

Related Majors: Computer Engineering, p. 104; Computer Science, p. 85.

SOFTWARE DEVELOPERS, SYSTEMS SOFTWARE

Research, design, develop, and test operating systems-level software, compilers, and network distribution software for medical, industrial, military, communications, aerospace, business, scientific, and general computing applications. Set operational specifications and formulate and analyze software requirements. May design embedded systems software. Apply principles and techniques of computer science, engineering, and mathematical analysis.

Annual Earnings. Average: $101,410. **Middle 50%:** $79,900–$126,880.

Employment Outlook. Workforce 2012: 405,000. **Projected Growth 2012–22:** 20.4%. **Projected Annual Openings:** 13,470.

Personality Type(s): Investigative–Conventional–Realistic. **Top Skills:** Mathematics; Communication; Thought-Processing. **Work Environment:** Indoors; sitting.

Typical Entry Requirements. Education: Bachelor's degree. **Work Experience:** None. **On-the-Job Training:** None.

Related Majors: Computer Engineering, p. 104; Computer Science, p. 85.

SOIL AND PLANT SCIENTISTS

Conduct research in breeding, physiology, production, yield, and management of crops and agricultural plants or trees, shrubs, and nursery stock, their growth in soils, and control of pests; or study the chemical, physical, biological, and mineralogical composition of soils as they relate to plant or crop growth. May classify and map soils and investigate effects of alternative practices on soil and crop productivity.

Annual Earnings. Average: $58,990. **Middle 50%:** $44,420–$75,620.

Employment Outlook. Workforce 2012: 16,300. **Projected Growth 2012–22:** 7.5%. **Projected Annual Openings**: 670.

Personality Type(s): Investigative–Realistic. **Top Skills:** Science; Thought-Processing; Mathematics; Communication; Technology/ Programming; Social; Management. **Work Environment:** Indoors; outdoors; sitting.

Typical Entry Requirements. Education: Bachelor's degree. **Work Experience:** None. **On-the-Job Training:** None.

Related Majors: Agronomy, p. 66.

SPECIAL EDUCATION TEACHERS, ALL OTHER

All special education teachers not listed separately.

Annual Earnings. Average: $49,970. **Middle 50%:** $39,790–$68,610.

Employment Outlook. Workforce 2012: 40,700. **Projected Growth 2012–22:** 9.5%. **Projected Annual Openings**: 1,080.

Personality Type(s): No data available. **Top Skills:** No data available. **Work Environment:** No data available.

Typical Entry Requirements. Education: Bachelor's degree. **Work Experience:** None. **On-the-Job Training:** Student teaching.

Related Majors: Special Education (see your state's requirements), p. 95.

JOB SPECIALIZATION: ADAPTED PHYSICAL EDUCATION SPECIALISTS

Provide individualized physical education instruction or services to children, youth, or adults with exceptional physical needs due to gross motor developmental delays or other impairments.

Personality Type(s): Social–Realistic. **Top Skills:** Communication; Thought-Processing; Technology/Programming; Social. **Work Environment:** Indoors; standing; walking and running; noisy; disease or infections.

SPECIAL EDUCATION TEACHERS, KINDERGARTEN AND ELEMENTARY SCHOOL

Teach elementary school subjects to educationally and physically handicapped students. Includes teachers who specialize and work with audibly and visually handicapped students and those who teach basic academic and life processes skills to the mentally impaired.

Annual Earnings. Average: $53,910. **Middle 50%:** $43,380–$67,710.

Employment Outlook. Workforce 2012: 194,600. **Projected Growth 2012–22:** 6.2%. **Projected Annual Openings:** 4,520.

Personality Type(s): Social–Artistic. **Top Skills:** No data available. **Work Environment:** No data available.

Typical Entry Requirements. Education: Bachelor's degree. **Work Experience:** None. **On-the-Job Training:** Student teaching.

Related Majors: Special Education (see your state's requirements), p. 95.

SPECIAL EDUCATION TEACHERS, MIDDLE SCHOOL

Teach middle school subjects to educationally and physically handicapped students. Includes teachers who specialize and work with audibly and visually handicapped students and those who teach basic academic and life processes skills to the mentally impaired.

Annual Earnings. Average: $56,300. **Middle 50%:** $45,400–$71,150.

Employment Outlook. Workforce 2012: 94,600. **Projected Growth 2012–22:** 5.2%. **Projected Annual Openings:** 2,110.

Personality Type(s): Social–Artistic. **Top Skills:** Social; Technology/Programming; Thought-Processing; Communication. **Work Environment:** Indoors; standing.

Typical Entry Requirements. Education: Bachelor's degree. **Work Experience:** None. **On-the-Job Training:** Student teaching.

Related Majors: Special Education (see your state's requirements), p. 95.

SPECIAL EDUCATION TEACHERS, PRESCHOOL

Teach preschool school subjects to educationally and physically handicapped students. Includes teachers who specialize and work with audibly and visually handicapped students and those who teach basic academic and life processes skills to the mentally impaired.

Annual Earnings. Average: $52,070. **Middle 50%:** $41,220–$66,840.

Employment Outlook. Workforce 2012: 22,300. **Projected Growth 2012–22:** 16.2%. **Projected Annual Openings:** 740.

Personality Type(s): Social–Artistic. **Top Skills:** No data available. **Work Environment:** No data available.

Typical Entry Requirements. Education: Bachelor's degree. **Work Experience:** None. **On-the-Job Training:** Student teaching.

Related Majors: Special Education (see your state's requirements), p. 95.

SPECIAL EDUCATION TEACHERS, SECONDARY SCHOOL

Teach secondary school subjects to educationally and physically handicapped students. Includes teachers who specialize and work with audibly and visually handicapped students and those who teach basic academic and life processes skills to the mentally impaired.

Annual Earnings. Average: $56,920. **Middle 50%:** $45,790–$72,370.

Employment Outlook. Workforce 2012: 131,300. **Projected Growth 2012–22:** 4.6%. **Projected Annual Openings:** 2,850.

Personality Type(s): Social–Investigative. **Top Skills:** Mathematics; Communication; Technology/Programming; Social; Thought-Processing. **Work Environment:** Indoors; standing; noisy.

Typical Entry Requirements. Education: Bachelor's degree. **Work Experience:** None. **On-the-Job Training:** Student teaching.

Related Majors: Special Education (see your state's requirements), p. 95.

SPEECH-LANGUAGE PATHOLOGISTS

Assess and treat persons with speech, language, voice, and fluency disorders. May select alternative communication systems and teach their use. May perform research related to speech and language problems.

Annual Earnings. Average: $70,810. **Middle 50%:** $55,660–$89,170.

Employment Outlook. Workforce 2012: 134,100. **Projected Growth 2012–22:** 19.4%. **Projected Annual Openings:** 4,620.

Personality Type(s): Social–Investigative–Artistic. **Top Skills:** Science; Communication; Mathematics; Social; Technology/Programming; Thought-Processing. **Work Environment:** Indoors; sitting; disease or infections.

Typical Entry Requirements. Education: Master's degree (in Speech-Language Pathology). **Work Experience:** None. **On-the-Job Training:** None.

Related Majors: Pre-Professional Health (or any major, plus courses required for entry to graduate program in speech-language pathology), p. 131.

STATISTICIANS

Develop or apply mathematical or statistical theory and methods to collect, organize, interpret, and summarize numerical data to provide usable information. May specialize in fields such as biostatistics, agricultural statistics, business statistics, or economic statistics. Includes mathematical and survey statisticians.

Annual Earnings. Average: $79,290. **Middle 50%:** $58,360–$103,870.

Employment Outlook. Workforce 2012: 27,600. **Projected Growth 2012–22:** 26.7%. **Projected Annual Openings**: 1,610.

Personality Type(s): Conventional–Investigative. **Top Skills:** Mathematics; Science; Communication; Thought-Processing. **Work Environment:** Indoors; sitting.

Typical Entry Requirements. Education: Master's degree (in Mathematics or Statistics). **Work Experience:** None. **On-the-Job Training:** None.

Related Majors: Mathematics, p. 122; Statistics (or any major, plus courses required for entry to master's program in mathematics or statistics), p. 139.

JOB SPECIALIZATION: BIOSTATISTICIANS

Develop and apply biostatistical theory and methods to the study of life sciences.

Personality Type(s): Investigative–Conventional. **Top Skills:** Science; Mathematics; Communication; Thought-Processing; Technology/Programming; Social; Management. **Work Environment:** Indoors; sitting.

JOB SPECIALIZATION: CLINICAL DATA MANAGERS

Apply knowledge of health-care and database management to analyze clinical data and to identify and report trends.

Personality Type(s): Conventional–Investigative. **Top Skills:** Mathematics; Technology/Programming; Social; Thought-Processing; Communication; Science; Management. **Work Environment:** Indoors; sitting; repetitive motions.

SURGEONS

Physicians who treat diseases, injuries, and deformities by invasive, minimally-invasive, or non-invasive surgical methods, such as using instruments, appliances, or by manual manipulation.

Annual Earnings. Average: No data available. **Middle 50%:** No data available.

Employment Outlook. Workforce 2012: 47,900. **Projected Growth 2012–22:** 23.2%. **Projected Annual Openings**: 2,310.

Personality Type(s): Investigative–Realistic–Social. **Top Skills:** Science; Thought-Processing; Communication; Social; Technology/Programming; Management; Mathematics. **Work Environment:** Indoors; standing; using hands; repetitive motions; disease or infections.

Typical Entry Requirements. Education: Professional degree (in Medicine). **Work Experience:** None. **On-the-Job Training:** Internship/residency.

Related Majors: Pre-Professional Health (or any major, plus courses required for entry to medical school), p. 131.

SURVEY RESEARCHERS

Plan, develop, or conduct surveys. May analyze and interpret the meaning of survey data, determine survey objectives, or suggest or test question wording. Includes social scientists who primarily design questionnaires or supervise survey teams.

Annual Earnings. Average: $47,720. **Middle 50%:** $27,990–$72,370.

Employment Outlook. Workforce 2012: 18,000. **Projected Growth 2012–22:** 17.6%. **Projected Annual Openings**: 560.

Personality Type(s): Investigative–Conventional–Enterprising. **Top Skills:** Science; Mathematics; Social; Thought-Processing; Communication; Technology/Programming; Management. **Work Environment:** Indoors; sitting.

Typical Entry Requirements. Education: Master's degree (in Marketing Research, Statistics, Survey Research, or a social science). **Work Experience:** None. **On-the-Job Training:** None.

Related Majors: Economics, p. 88; Statistics (or any major, plus courses required for entry to master's program in economics, marketing research, survey research, statistics, or a social science), p. 139.

TAX EXAMINERS AND COLLECTORS AND REVENUE AGENTS

Determine tax liability or collect taxes from individuals or business firms according to prescribed laws and regulations.

Annual Earnings. Average: $50,610. **Middle 50%:** $38,780–$69,550.

Employment Outlook. Workforce 2012: 69,500. **Projected Growth 2012–22:** -3.9%. **Projected Annual Openings**: 2,390.

Personality Type(s): Conventional–Enterprising. **Top Skills:** Mathematics; Communication; Social. **Work Environment:** Indoors; sitting; repetitive motions.

Typical Entry Requirements. Education: Bachelor's degree. **Work Experience:** None. **On-the-Job Training:** Moderate-term on-the-job training.

Related Majors: Accounting, p. 73.

TRAINING AND DEVELOPMENT MANAGERS

Plan, direct, or coordinate the training and development activities and staff of an organization.

Annual Earnings. Average: $98,810. **Middle 50%:** $74,860–$131,820.

Employment Outlook. Workforce 2012: 28,600. **Projected Growth 2012–22:** 11.2%. **Projected Annual Openings**: 1,070.

Personality Type(s): Enterprising–Social. **Top Skills:** Management; Thought-Processing; Social; Communication; Mathematics. **Work Environment:** Indoors; sitting.

Typical Entry Requirements. Education: Bachelor's degree. **Work Experience:** 5 years or more. **On-the-Job Training:** None.

Related Majors: Business Management and Administration, p. 74; Human Resources Management, p. 77.

TRAINING AND DEVELOPMENT SPECIALISTS

Design and conduct training and development programs to improve individual and organizational performance. May analyze training needs.

Annual Earnings. Average: $56,850. **Middle 50%:** $41,820–$75,610.

Employment Outlook. Workforce 2012: 228,800. **Projected Growth 2012–22:** 15.5%. **Projected Annual Openings**: 7,720.

Personality Type(s): Social–Artistic–Conventional. **Top Skills:** Social; Communication; Thought-Processing; Management; Mathematics; Science. **Work Environment:** Indoors; sitting.

Typical Entry Requirements. Education: Bachelor's degree. **Work Experience:** Less than 5 years. **On-the-Job Training:** None.

Related Majors: Human Resources Management, p. 77.

TRANSPORTATION, STORAGE, AND DISTRIBUTION MANAGERS

Annual Earnings. Average: $83,890. **Middle 50%:** $64,080–$109,960.

Employment Outlook. Workforce 2012: 105,200. **Projected Growth 2012–22:** 4.9%. **Projected Annual Openings**: 2,910.

Typical Entry Requirements. Education: High school diploma or equivalent. **Work Experience:** 5 years or more. **On-the-Job Training:** None.

Related Majors: Business Management and Administration, p. 74.

JOB SPECIALIZATION: LOGISTICS MANAGERS

Plan, direct, or coordinate purchasing, warehousing, distribution, forecasting, customer service, or planning services. Manage logistics personnel and logistics systems and direct daily operations.

Personality Type(s): Enterprising–Conventional. **Top Skills:** Management; Thought-Processing; Technology/Programming; Social; Mathematics; Communication. **Work Environment:** Indoors; sitting.

JOB SPECIALIZATION: STORAGE AND DISTRIBUTION MANAGERS

Plan, direct, or coordinate the storage or distribution operations within an organization or the activities of organizations that are engaged in storing or distributing materials or products.

Personality Type(s): Enterprising–Conventional. **Top Skills:** Management; Social; Thought-Processing; Mathematics; Communication. **Work Environment:** Indoors; standing.

JOB SPECIALIZATION: TRANSPORTATION MANAGERS

Plan, direct, or coordinate the transportation operations within an organization or the activities of organizations that provide transportation services.

Personality Type(s): Enterprising–Conventional. **Top Skills:** Management; Thought-Processing; Technology/Programming; Social; Mathematics; Communication. **Work Environment:** Indoors; outdoors; sitting; using hands; repetitive motions; noisy.

VETERINARIANS

Diagnose, treat, or research diseases and injuries of animals. Includes veterinarians who conduct research and development, inspect livestock, or care for pets and companion animals.

Annual Earnings. Average: $86,640. **Middle 50%:** $69,020–$111,960.

Employment Outlook. Workforce 2012: 70,300. **Projected Growth 2012–22:** 12.0%. **Projected Annual Openings:** 3,100.

Personality Type(s): Investigative–Realistic. **Top Skills:** Science; Thought-Processing; Technology/Programming; Social; Management; Communication; Mathematics. **Work Environment:** Indoors; standing; using hands; noisy; contaminants; radiation; disease or infections; minor burns, cuts, bites, or stings.

Typical Entry Requirements. Education: Professional degree (in Veterinary Medicine). **Work Experience:** None. **On-the-Job Training:** None.

Related Majors: Pre-Professional Health (or any major, plus courses required for entry to veterinary school), p. 131.

WEB DEVELOPERS

Design, create, and modify websites. Analyze user needs to implement website content, graphics, performance, and capacity. May integrate websites with other computer applications. May convert written, graphic, audio, and video components to compatible web formats by using software designed to facilitate the creation of web and multimedia content.

Annual Earnings. Average: $63,160. **Middle 50%:** $44,550–$85,270.

Employment Outlook. Workforce 2012: 141,400. **Projected Growth 2012–22:** 20.1%. **Projected Annual Openings**: 5,070.

Personality Type(s): Conventional–Investigative–Realistic. **Top Skills:** Science; Technology/Programming; Thought-Processing; Social; Management; Installation; Communication; Mathematics. **Work Environment:** Indoors; sitting; using hands; repetitive motions.

Typical Entry Requirements. Education: Associate's degree. **Work Experience:** None. **On-the-Job Training:** None.

Related Majors: Computer Science, p. 85.

WRITERS AND AUTHORS

Originate and prepare written material, such as scripts, stories, advertisements, and other material.

Annual Earnings. Average: $57,750. **Middle 50%:** $40,130–$84,190.

Employment Outlook. Workforce 2012: 129,100. **Projected Growth 2012–22:** 3.0%. **Projected Annual Openings**: 3,180.

Typical Entry Requirements. Education: Bachelor's degree. **Work Experience:** None. **On-the-Job Training:** Moderate-term on-the-job training.

Related Majors: Communication, p. 84; English, p. 111; Journalism, p. 119.

JOB SPECIALIZATION: COPY WRITERS

Write advertising copy for use by publication or broadcast media to promote sale of goods and services.

Personality Type(s): Enterprising–Artistic. **Top Skills:** Social; Communication. **Work Environment:** Indoors; sitting.

JOB SPECIALIZATION: POETS, LYRICISTS, AND CREATIVE WRITERS

Create original written works, such as scripts, essays, prose, poetry, or song lyrics, for publication or performance.

Personality Type(s): Artistic–Investigative. **Top Skills:** Communication; Thought-Processing; Social. **Work Environment:** Indoors; sitting; using hands; repetitive motions.

KEY POINTS OF CHAPTER 7

- ❯ Make note of the occupations that seem like a good fit for you.
- ❯ When you consider a career goal, don't forget what it takes to reach the goal. Look at the requirements for the related major, and be sure to note whether additional education beyond the bachelor's is necessary.
- ❯ The information here is based on averages and on what is most common. Regional variations and exceptions occur.

CHAPTER 8

DECIDING AND IMPLEMENTING

Now that you have looked at various majors and their related occupations, it's time to make a tentative decision. Then you can begin the process of implementing your decision.

GUIDELINES FOR DECIDING

Probably no college major will be perfectly satisfying for you. Everyone enrolled in a major finds aspects they like and others they dislike. Your task now is to find a major for which the good characteristics heavily outweigh the bad.

In this chapter, a Major Decision-Making Checklist serves as a scorecard for evaluating majors. You may have already marked up your Hot List in chapter 5 to indicate which majors have the greatest appeal. But this checklist leads you through a systematic process that will help you identify the most promising major of all and understand why it seems like your best bet.

Before you get started, understand that the checklist is only a model, and you may modify it to serve your needs better. For example, the checklist is based on the assumption that you have narrowed down your thinking to two or three possible majors. Therefore, it has three columns for majors that you are considering. If you have more than three in mind, feel free to add as many columns as necessary.

Now, follow these steps to complete the checklist:

〉 In the blanks at the head of each column (under "Major #1," and so forth), write the names of the top majors you are now considering.

〉 **For the "Fit with my personality" row:** Go back to chapter 2 and see what you decided about your personality type(s) on page 36. Now, for each major, look at what chapter 7 says about the personality type(s) of the related occupations. If the occupations are mostly good matches in terms of personality, write a plus sign (+) in the blank space. Note that a perfect match is not necessary; it may be a good match if only the primary personality type of the occupations matches your primary personality type, or a fairly good match if it's a match between a primary and a secondary type. If there is little or no overlap of personality types, write a minus sign (–) in the blank.

〉 **For the "Fit with my skills" row:** Go back to chapter 3 and look at the top skills you identified on pp. 46-47. Now, for each major, look at the skills required for the related occupations, as identified in chapter 7. If there is a good amount of overlap between your top skills and those specified for the occupation, write a plus sign in the blank space. If there's little or no overlap, write a minus sign.

〉 **For the "Fit with favorite high school courses" row:** Look at the beginning of chapter 4 (pp. 52-53), where you identified the three high school courses that gave you the most enjoyment and the best grades. Now, for each major, look at the "Usual High School Prerequisites" listed in chapter 6. Write a plus or minus sign to indicate how well these courses match your favorites.

〉 **For the "Appeal of college courses" row:** For each major, look at the "Courses Studied in College" listed in chapter 6. Think about how much you would enjoy these courses and how well you might do in them. (It's understandable that your estimate at this time may be very rough.) Write a plus or minus sign to indicate your best estimate of how appealing this program of study looks to you now.

> **For the "Appeal of specializations, related occupations, and career paths" row:** For each major, think about whether one or more of the specializations, related occupations, and career paths listed in chapter 6 seem appealing to you. Make a judgment about whether to give the major a plus or a minus. These ratings will be even rougher guesses than the ratings in the previous row. It's difficult to predict your future job reliably; the major may lead you to a career path not even listed here.

> **For the "Related occupations" rows:** In chapter 7, look at the facts for the occupations related to each major. For each major, write a plus or minus sign to indicate your level of comfort with the facts listed for the related occupations. If you have a strong preference for one occupation over the others linked to the major, indicate your reactions to only that one occupation.

At the bottom of the checklist, you'll notice that there are three rows that are not labeled. You may use these rows to rate any other characteristics of the majors that are missing from the checklist. For example, maybe at your college one of the majors has a requirement (such as a particular field experience) for which you have a strong preference or dislike. Or maybe you have strong feelings about the kinds of people you have met who are enrolled in this major or who are working in related occupations. Feel free to add any other characteristics that are important to you and for which you can get reliable information about the majors.

MAJOR DECISION-MAKING CHECKLIST

Characteristic	Major #1	Major #2	Major #3
Fit with my personality			

MAJOR DECISION-MAKING CHECKLIST

Fit with my skills			
Fit with favorite high school courses			
Appeal of college courses			
Appeal of specializations, related occupations, and career paths			
Related occupations			
Work tasks			
Earnings			
Employment outlook			
Work environment			
Typical entry requirements			

Now that you have filled out the checklist, look at how the majors compare according to the plus and minus signs you have given them. Don't simply compute the total number of plus and minus signs, because these factors do not all deserve equal weight. The marks you give to the first three rows should probably carry the most weight.

If you have time, gather information from some other sources and make any necessary adjustments to your first estimates in the checklist:

❭ Talk to people who are (or were) enrolled in the major. Ask them about their experiences—what they liked and disliked about it.

❭ Talk to an academic advisor who specializes in the field. Get detailed information about the requirements for the major. This conversation may reveal a lot of information that the college catalog or the departmental website leaves unsaid.

❭ If there is a student organization for people in the major (or for a career goal associated with the major), attend a meeting. See how interesting the conversation is and how well you fit in with the members you meet.

❭ Get detailed information about related occupations from the *Occupational Outlook Handbook* (www.bls.gov/ooh/).

❭ Talk to people working in the career paths that the major leads to. (Your college's alumni association may help you make these contacts.) Ask them what a good day and a bad day on the job are like. Ask them to suggest the best ways to prepare for the job: the degree to get, the courses to take, the internships to experience, and so forth.

❭ Visit a worksite of a related occupation. Find out what it looks like, sounds like, feels like, smells like. Get some impressions of the kinds of people who work there.

IMPLEMENTING YOUR DECISION

Once you have decided on a major, you need to implement your decision.

If you are a **high school student**, you need to deal with these issues:

❭ **Appropriate courses.** You should be taking courses related to the major. These may be prerequisites for entering the major or may just give you a head start in preparing for it. Perhaps a relevant summer-school program is available. Your experience in related courses will help you confirm that you enjoy academic work in this field.

❭ **Choosing a college.** When you apply to college, you should choose one that offers your targeted major. Ideally, the college should have a good reputation for educating people in this field and for the job-entry success of graduates. You might talk to employers and ask which colleges turn out the best job candidates. Or you might look at LinkedIn (www.linkedin.com), search for a job title, and make a note of the college backgrounds of successful workers.

❭ **Enrichment activities.** Get involved in a student organization or volunteer service related to your intended major. Get a part-time or summer job in a work environment similar to the one where graduates of the major work. If you can't get a job there, visit a worksite and talk to people about their job. Ask them for suggestions about how to use your time in college effectively.

If you are a **college student**, you need to follow the policies of the college and of the department offering the major. You also need to deal with these issues:

❭ **Entry requirements.** Some majors have prerequisite courses, or your GPA must exceed a certain minimum. If so, are you on track to meet these requirements?

❭ **Paperwork.** To formalize your decision, you will probably need the signature of your academic advisor or of an advisor from the office of the academic department offering the major.

❭ **Planning for courses and for other requirements.** When you meet with the academic advisor, you should plan when and how you will meet the requirements for the degree. Map out the rest of your college education, year by year. Your plans may be sketchy in places, because course offerings often change from year to year, and it may not be possible to know now exactly when certain courses will be available. Nevertheless, you should get at least a rough idea of when you will take key courses and how you will meet any other requirements, such as supervised work experience.

❭ **Enrichment activities.** Start thinking about pursuing optional courses or extracurricular activities that will enhance your education and expand your skills. For example, your department may offer an honors program or the option of a senior project. You may want to get active in a student organization or volunteer service related to the major or to a targeted occupation. You may start planning for a relevant internship, summer job, or semester abroad.

Try not to stress over this decision and the planning that it requires. Talk to juniors and seniors in the major or—better yet—alumni who have graduated with the major. They will have suggestions that can smooth your way and calm your anxieties about the road ahead.

Good luck with your decision, but remember: It's not simply a matter of luck. You have to make your decision work out.

KEY POINTS OF CHAPTER 8

❱ No major is perfectly satisfying all the time, but you can find one that has many good features and few bad ones.

❱ When you consider the various aspects of a major, you should give greater weight to factors that you are already competent to judge, such as the relationship of the major to a favorite high school course, and less weight to more remote factors, such as your future satisfaction with a specific occupation.

❱ To implement your decision and get the most out of your college experience, you will need to make plans for both academic and extracurricular activities.

APPENDIX

DEFINITIONS OF PERSONALITY TYPES AND SKILLS

THE SIX HOLLAND PERSONALITY TYPES

Chapter 2 helps you think about your personality type and which college majors might suit you. The six personality types in chapter 2 were developed by John S. Holland. Here are definitions of the six types, expressed in terms of work activities (not academic pursuits) that suit these types:

> **Realistic** personalities like work activities that include practical, hands-on problems and solutions. They enjoy dealing with plants, animals, and real-world materials like wood, tools, and machinery. They enjoy outside work. Often they do not like occupations that mainly involve doing paperwork or working closely with others.

> **Investigative** personalities like work activities that have to do with ideas and thinking more than with physical activity. They like to search for facts and figure out problems mentally rather than to persuade or lead people.

> **Artistic** personalities like work activities that deal with the artistic side of things, such as forms, designs, and patterns. They like self-

expression in their work. They prefer settings where work can be done without following a clear set of rules.

)   **Social** personalities like work activities that assist others and promote learning and personal development. They prefer to communicate more than to work with objects, machines, or data. They like to teach, to give advice, to help, or otherwise to be of service to people.

)   **Enterprising** personalities like work activities having to do with starting up and carrying out projects, especially business ventures. They like persuading and leading people and making decisions. They like taking risks for profit. These personalities prefer action rather than thought.

)   **Conventional** personalities like work activities that follow set procedures and routines. They prefer working with data and details rather than with ideas. They prefer work in which there are precise standards rather than work in which you have to judge things by yourself. These personalities like working where the lines of authority are clear.

THE SPECIFIC AND GENERIC SKILLS

Chapter 3 helps you think about your skills. The quick assessment asks you to rate yourself on nine specialized skills, and then you see generic skills that are matched to the specialized skills. This matching is the result of a statistical analysis of the ratings of occupations in the O*NET database.

The following table shows which specialized skills (in addition to those used in the quick assessment) are matched to each generic skill:

SPECIALIZED SKILL IN O*NET DATABASE	GENERIC SKILL MATCHED TO SPECIALIZED SKILL
Reading Comprehension	Communication
Active Listening	Communication
Speaking	Communication
Writing	Communication
Management of Financial Resources	Management
Management of Material Resources	Management
Management of Personnel Resources	Management
Time Management	Management
Mathematics	Mathematics
Science	Science
Service Orientation	Social
Coordination	Social
Instructing	Social
Negotiation	Social
Persuasion	Social
Social Perceptiveness	Social
Equipment Maintenance	Equipment Use/Maintenance
Operation and Control	Equipment Use/Maintenance
Operation Monitoring	Equipment Use/Maintenance
Quality Control Analysis Skills	Equipment Use/Maintenance
Repairing	Equipment Use/Maintenance

SPECIALIZED SKILL IN O*NET DATABASE	GENERIC SKILL MATCHED TO SPECIALIZED SKILL
Troubleshooting	Equipment Use/Maintenance
Installation	Installation
Programming	Technology/Programming
Technology Design	Technology/Programming
Active Learning	Thought-Processing
Complex Problem Solving	Thought-Processing
Critical Thinking	Thought-Processing
Judgment and Decision Making	Thought-Processing
Learning Strategies	Thought-Processing
Monitoring	Thought-Processing
Operations Analysis	Thought-Processing
Systems Analysis	Thought-Processing
Systems Evaluation	Thought-Processing